DO YOU LOVE ME?
Ministry in Today's Church

Dominic Grassi

THE THOMAS MORE PRESS
Chicago, Illinois

ISBN 0-88347-254-6

Contents

Dedication

Do You Love Me? is dedicated to Jim, Tom, Beth and Dennis, Sue and Bernie. Our praying together has helped me more than anything else understand my call to ministry and theirs.

Acknowledgments

I would like to thank Thomas More Press for the invitation to write *Do You Love Me?* I thank the people of St. John De La Salle Parish, the students, families, and faculty of Quigley Seminary South, the people of St. Germaine Parish and most of all, the people of St. Josaphat Parish whom I now serve, for allowing me to be minister to and with them, and who have taught me what I share in this book. Thanks, too, to Father Dennis Geaney who encouraged me to write, and Fr. Jack Egan, who challenges me to be all that I can as a priest. Mrs. Ruby Alexander challenged and helped me focus many of the ideas in this book. And finally, Ms. Sandi Smith prepared the manuscript, spending many long hours in front of a computer terminal.

Preface

THE journey that was the writing of *Do You Love Me?* was at times a most painful one. The words I would write in the quiet of my room after midnight would often come back and haunt me as I attempted to minister to the people of St. Josaphat Parish. Occasionally I would drop the premise of this book into a conversation I was sharing at various gatherings. And then I would wait for a reaction. After a while an identifiable pattern of responses began to develop. Priests could be divided into two groups: those, most of them in difficult assignments and working hard, who picked up the notion of loving people as central to their call and would excitedly amplify it; and those who were cynical and extremely patronizing to the premise and to me.

Others involved in pastoral ministry, especially those who were not ordained, seemed hopeful and looked forward to the recognition and validation of their work the book might offer. They feel very little support in what they are doing.

Women's responses were the most painful — not those working on the fringe or the angry individuals, but the dedicated, hard-working, faith-filled women. Sadly, their loss may well be recorded by history as more damaging to the church and certainly more preventable than the current declining numbers of male, celibate priests.

Part of the time I was writing this book coincided with the finality of the massive church closings in Detroit and the advent of similar closings in my own Archdiocese of Chicago. Morale has never been lower. Rural dioceses as well are feeling the crunch of not having enough priests. But instead of growth in other ministries, confusion reigns as mixed messages are being given regarding priestless parishes and liturgies and the role of the non-ordained in the church. The knee-jerk reaction, the lack of vision and leadership, the absence of courage among the hierarchy is pitifully sad. But to sit back and blame them for all that is happening in the Church is no better than, and as unproductive as, the parishioners who complain and do nothing and then blame the pastor for their parish's problems.

It is our church and no one else's. We have to believe this. We must also believe that good ministry can and will fill our churches, schools, and halls. More importantly, it will empower people to be church for each other. These can be exciting times. We may no longer have the funds to construct the large edifices of faith our parents and grandparents built. But we can build strong and vibrant communities of believers who come together in faith wanting to worship together, welcomed and welcoming. This can be a time of tremendous growth rather than decline and closure for the church in America. It is up to us and the leadership we're willing to provide.

And so this book is written to celebrate and support those who are involved in serving the people of God. It is meant

DO YOU LOVE ME?

to challenge but also to affirm. It is my hope that those who take the time to read these pages will find in them some strength to continue. There is no time to be afraid. There is no reason to be afraid. Jesus did not leave the disciples with a question, but rather with the firm assurance that he would be with us, be with his church always, yes, even to the end of time.

Completed
November 12, 1989 The Feast of St. Josaphat,
Patron of Christian Unity

Introduction

THE more I read the Gospels, the more I am struck by the number of questions that are asked. Surprisingly, Jesus seems to ask as many as the disciples and the Pharisees and the other lesser players put together. If Jesus and his public ministry and his drawing others to him elicited so many questions it is little wonder that so many questions arise in the church today.

Quite simply, the church is currently experiencing an explosion of ministries. Being involved in the church has become a very complex undertaking. There are no models out there for us to follow. We're creating what we mean by ministry and service as we go along. It's a bumpy ride.

Back in the 50s, if my memory of those simpler times hasn't faded, there was a simpler structure. Sister Principal ruled the school and the teaching Sisters were positioned directly under her. And under them were the barely tolerated, occasional lay teachers. However, when the young associate pastor came on the scene to teach religion or hand out report cards, he was clearly now in charge, although authority may have been relinquished to him begrudgingly by the Sisters. The older associate, while more remote, held more power. You could tell by the way the younger priest deferred to him. At solemn high masses the older of the two would be deacon to the younger's sub-deacon. Of course the celebrant was the pastor. It was with him that all control ultimately rested, be he the jovial friend of all or the more distant keeper of the cash box keys. And that was about it in a parish except when the bishop came around asking Confirmation questions. In those days, ushers ushered and secretaries did what secretaries do. There were no Eucharistic Ministers, no Pastoral Associates, no Ministers of Care, nor any Lectors. Ministers of Music were called organists. All societies from the Holy Name to the Girl Scouts had priest moderators to keep them from falling into the deep pit of heresy and to lead opening and closing prayers.

Some would look back fondly on those days. Others would find them as boring as Mamie Eisenhower. The only questions being asked were along the lines of "Father, I swallowed some toothpaste this morning. Did I break my fast? Can I go to Communion?"

Well, the church certainly isn't that way anymore, nor should it be. But with what have we replaced it?

Recently I attended Mass in a university town in Indiana. As I walked in the door of the church I was quickly greeted by men and women handing me bulletins and song books and orders of liturgy. Each was wearing a big smile and a badge more than three inches in diameter proclaiming that they were "Ministers of Hospitality." After being led hospitably to my seat, I studied the parish bulletin that had been handed to me and found that it listed a full eighteen staff members (and ten different phone numbers to reach them). The cantor, wearing some sort of ceremonial robe, introduced the opening hymn. The procession that began,

DO YOU LOVE ME?

was led by three young altar servers dressed like white-hooded monks. They were followed by eight Eucharistic ministers marching two by two wearing matching crosses four inches long. The lectors, with robes similar in style but different in color than the cantor's gown followed, two of them, one carrying the book of readings over her head as though ready to beat someone with it. Two deacons with identical stoles led the priest who was last in the procession up the aisle. At the front of the church, in the area reserved for music, a choir of about thirty, all robed like the lectors and cantor, but with still different colors, sang. And let's not forget the organist who had on a robe with its own special hue. One couldn't help but be impressed.

After the homily, fifteen parishioners came forward to receive a special pin recognizing them as newly commissioned ministers of care. It was presented to them by someone identified as a pastoral associate who appeared out of the sacristy dressed, you guessed it, in a robe unique in design and also wearing a cross. I found myself looking around to see if there was anybody left in the pews with me who didn't have some special designation that somehow would set them apart.

As courageous people understand and accept their baptismal commitment to share in the priesthood of Jesus Christ, and therefore are attempting to be church to others, and as their work is finally recognized and given its proper space to grow, good things happen in the church. At the same time, as tasks expand and sometimes compete or threaten, there is a tremendous amount of pain, misunderstanding, and hurt being felt by many. And that same good is quickly being overshadowed.

15

Dominic Grassi

The Second Vatican Council, prompted by the Spirit, and by an elderly pope who, in his soul's journey, realized he had nothing to lose and the church had everything to gain, courageously opened doors too long locked to all but male celibates. In a brief flash of time, a mere moment in history, the church caught up to a world that was quickly leaving it behind. It goes without saying that such rapid change left some people disturbed and others militant. After a period of confusion, those forces are regathering with the support and blessing, sometimes public and, more than we'd like to admit, private, of some in Rome and their appointees who find their own world being challenged by these changes. How dare those Americans, they find themselves saying over their Sambucca in a cafe near the Piazza Minerva, take up a collection in their churches to support women's roles in the church and call it Mary's Pence in place of the sacred Peter's Pence collection?

This is a crucial time for the church. And unless those of us who love it can find some common ground and come together, the forces that would take us back to a church that can never exist again will get the upper hand. And it is the people who we are privileged to serve that will suffer in confusion and in abandonment.

Everywhere we hear of the growing crisis of a shortage of priests. Some see this almost as a punishment, the fault of all that has happened since Vatican II. Others dance gleefully, if not prematurely, on the grave of the male, celibate priesthood and the hierarchical church for which it stood. Others feel sadly helpless about it all.

But, is anyone bothering to notice the tremendous and

16

frightening loss of talented women and men who have left the church in pain, anger, and fatigue? Instead of saying "See how those Christians love one another," people are ignoring us and reading instead about how to heal themselves with crystals and with Shirley MacLaine's help. Our intersquad fighting has not only demoralized us and divided us, but also has made us irrelevent to many who really do need us. Bishops forbidding women's feet to be washed on Holy Thursday make the headlines. The person bathing a bed-ridden senior parishioner does not.

If we don't come together, the whole church is going to come apart. This book will attempt the not too easy task of trying to convince everyone who is involved in the work of being church to put down their defenses and open their arms to embrace and support each other and the people they serve. All of us need to ask each other questions and listen to the questions being asked us. We need not concern ourselves with answers. They will come if we listen and pose the right questions. We need to be open and not defensive.

The image of the "professional Christian" coming in and doing his or her thing, a solitary Shane-like figure and then riding off into the sunset doesn't make sense anymore. Effective helping is too visible, too public. The isolated practitioner loses perspective and ultimately the ability to genuinely model the Gospel message. If we cannot love others who are ministering along side of us, how can we love those who are looking to find Jesus' presence in us?

Anyone who has ever tried to concentrate on another's problems and concerns just after being confronted by someone in anger knows how difficult it is to listen and be compassionate. It's better to cancel and reschedule the encounter. Anger, fear and frustration block our ability to care and love. If we are constantly attacking or being attacked by each other there are no energies left to love and serve those people who need us.

Many of us in the church have betrayed its sacred trust and because of our fears and jealousies, because of our humanity, we have betrayed Jesus as really as Peter did when he denied Him three times. And so like Peter we are given the opportunity and must answer the same question posed to him by the resurrected Jesus, "Do you love me?" Peter's affirmative answer washed away his anxiety and guilt in denying the Lord and gave him a new beginning. Let our love of our people we are called to serve in whatever capacity be our common ground. Let that love unite us. And so let it re-unite a fractured church. Let our energies turn from the draining infighting and jockeying for position that is taking place. For if we truly love the people we serve, that love will empower the Spirit of God to once again animate the church. And let's do it before it is too late.

CHAPTER 1

"Do you love me?"

What it means to love

A WHILE ago, I was delighted to receive an invitation from the Dean of Students, a layman at a college seminary, to be a part of his students' final exam at the end of the term. He had been teaching an elective class in basic business practice. (It's about time they were teaching such courses in a seminary, I might add.) He wanted me to come in and describe what I had done to "market" the parish at which I was pastoring in a rapidly gentrifying Chicago neighborhood. He would grade the seminarians on the questions that they asked and on the comments that they made. I quickly accepted the offer. After all, who can resist talking about oneself?

So, in my own mind, I dazzled the class with my statistics. Registrations, Mass attendance, sacraments, school population, collections—all were up significantly. With no little pride I handed out my newly printed "Guide to Parish Activities," registration cards, and parish brochures. I was at my best. By God, if it's a priest who's into marketing his product they want, they were going to get one they wouldn't be able to forget! I finished my presentation and after a dramatic pause I struck a very scholarly sitting posture on the edge of the desk to await their awe-filled questions.

The first hand went up somewhat hesitantly. Maybe I

should have held back a little, I thought. It all may have been too much for these young minds. Obviously, I was not anticipating his question. After politely telling me that all my figures were impressive and my hand-outs very nice, he asked me why I had not talked about my feelings toward the people. He wanted to know if they were just numbers and statistics to me or real flesh and blood. And could I spend a little time speaking to what the people meant to me and if I really cared about them, and wasn't that really ministry and service, and not all the incidentals that I had just presented to the class?

Needless to say, I was duly chastised. Trying to recover, I told him and the class that his comments were a most funny coincidence, indeed. Would they believe that I was planning to write a book on that very topic, loving the people you serve, and that I should have framed all that I had presented to them in that context.

Wise and sensitive young man with the courage to ask a real question and not worry about the teacher ready to grade you, I hope you choose some form of service for your life work. It must come naturally to you. You understood that without love, we, especially ministers, are nothing at all, just as St. Paul says. And I hope you received an "A" from your teacher. After all, good ministry is good business.

Serving others can appear to take up a lot of time and often does. But ministers are very often busy doing things that aren't essential to their being Christian. A wise but hurting pastor lamented that since he had lost his associate pastor (and there wasn't a replacement), people came to him less, fearing he did not have the time for them. How sad! That is why it is most important not to lose sight of the fact that

DO YOU LOVE ME?

we need constantly to make the time necessary to communicate the love we feel for people. And so we need to answer the following questions: first of all, what does it mean to love those whom we serve? Secondly, how can we find the time to do it? And, finally, concretely, how do we show the love that we do have?

Perhaps the most misunderstood and overused word in our culture is "love." It can mean anything from the physical act of human sexual expression, "going all the way," to a strong attraction to or desire for something like a brand of shampoo or a particular automobile. We use that same word "love" to describe our feelings about a boy or girl friend, our dog, a movie we've just seen, or a pair of shoes in a store window. Is it the limitations inherent in our language that force us to overuse that word or do we choose to limit our language by misusing the word so badly? In either case, what love really means gets lost.

So what does it really mean to say that we must love the people to whom we minister? On the most basic level, it means stripping away all that is excess and seeing, as Jesus was so capable of doing, into the essence of others. And when this happens we must be sufficiently vulnerable to allow the core of our very selves to touch and embrace intimately that other person. It is empathy, or "feeling with" another person, taken a step further to include accepting, affirming and helping to complete others without judging them.

A highly successful parish began a week-long celebration of its remodeled church with an ecumenical prayer service led by the pastoral associate. Local clergy, rabbis and pastors were invited to attend along with the parish community. In a genuinely caring gesture, a special invitation went out to the street people whose presence was only barely tolerated by most in that upscale neighborhood. No one anticipated the fact that the street people would select a spokesperson to represent them and that he would bring a single red rose up the center aisle at an unscheduled moment in the ceremony. The pastoral associate allowed the well rehearsed and orchestrated ceremony to pause momentarily. She accepted the gift with all the warmth that was intended and allowed a rather rambling, incoherent, but genuine speech to accompany the presentation. Her response, which could have only come from the heart, let the street people know not only that their gift was gratefully accepted, but, more importantly, they were and always would be accepted as an important and essential part of that parish community. She was neither patronizing nor condescending in her response. The love that was exchanged between her and the presenter of the rose sparked what would have otherwise been an over-rehearsed, self-conscious ceremony.

Loving others means taking risks. Ushers were ready to whisk away that unscheduled speaker. But if that had happened, it would have been everyone's embarrassing loss. Could he have said or done something potentially harmful? Most likely that would not have happened. And even if it had, the ceremony would have recovered and survived. It was worth taking the chance. Risk taking shows our own vulnerability, makes us more human, and allows others to respond to us because we are like them. They can identify with us.

The ultimate risk we take is being rejected. And once we

DO YOU LOVE ME?

learn that rejection still may happen no matter how hard we try to protect ourselves, the more open we can become. The most Christian among us will not, cannot reach everyone. We can only offer the gift of ourselves to others to be accepted, embraced, ignored, or rejected.

Loving others means taking people where they are and not where we or society think that they should be. A youth minister was hired by a parish that gave him his own space in a basement as a drop-in center for teens. He decorated it, carpeted it, installed a stereo, put up posters, and put together a calendar of events and activities. Unfortunately no one showed up for his meetings. No matter what he did or scheduled, the teens just did not feel comfortable in coming to the rectory. One night, he finally locked up the room early, and went out looking for his teens. He found them in the church parking lot a half a block away. And once he saw the thirty or forty teens hanging around there, he knew that this was where his work would have to begin.

When we take people where they are, it shows a genuine respect for them and an openness to listen to them and their agenda, not just be concerned about our own. It shows that we care. And out of that care love can grow.

And so it follows that loving others means allowing them to touch our hearts and change us. It means being vulnerable yet unafraid. We must remember that love is a relationship and that means that it takes two people and that it goes both ways.

Loving others also means not being afraid to feel what they are feeling. This means being open to them and trying to understand where they are coming from and what has brought them to this moment in their lives. A parishioner decided to visit an elderly lady whose daughters were able to find time to be with their mother only five or six times a year. As one who genuinely cared, she was successful because she brought her own experiences of pain and fear from numerous hospitalizations and her strong feelings for a recently deceased grandmother to the relationship. By bringing back feelings from her own past, she was able to understand a widowed, lonely and sick person. But it is an understatement to say that doing that was risky. It was worth the risk. She was obviously successful in helping her elderly friend and in so doing most certainly helped herself.

It is very difficult to pinpoint concretely what it means to love those to whom we are called to minister. The above ideas and examples should at least get us thinking about it. Each of our own responses in love will be as unique and as special as we are. How and why each one of us loves will vary. That we must love is undeniable.

Now, how do we find the time to love? It has to be a priority in our lives. There are only so many hours a day that a person can give to others. Some may have more time than others, granted. But no matter how much time people in ministry are able to give, few feel as though they have enough. The question becomes clearly one of quality, then and not quantity.

There is a need to make sure that the time we give to ministry is spent doing just that and not other work. In a parish that was still being served by a family-run funeral home where the undertakers knew everybody in the neighborhood, a long-time, very active parishioner died suddenly leaving a lot of people touched by his death. The undertaker presupposed that the pastor would be celebrating the Mass of the Resurrection. But at the wake the pastor informed the surprised undertaker that he could not possibly do the funeral the next day because he had to install a new doorknob! Both professionally and personally the undertaker felt free to challenge him. And although the pastor muttered a lame excuse that he couldn't entrust the job to his maintenance engineer, and everything fell on his shoulders, he evidently felt sufficiently moved to be the celebrant the next day. Too often we fool ourselves with busy work that isn't genuinely, people centered. Chances are better than average that if what we are doing keeps us from interacting with people when they need us, it isn't really important.

Job descriptions, available time and energy, as well as priorities all have to be constantly reevaluated. Flexibility is needed. People cannot keep adding activities to their schedules without it eventually affecting them and their performance. But there is a caution here. We need to make sure that we don't make the excuse of being too busy as a way of avoiding the tasks that we have committed ourselves to do. Talk about burn-out among those who help others is fashionable these days. It will be discussed at length in a later chapter. Suffice it to note here as a caution that persons can never suffer burn-out if they have never been on fire.

A wonderfully faith-filled married couple were initially very comfortable with the ministry in their lives. Hers centered on teaching and his on being a lawyer. Involvement in their parish was also an important part of their lives. But having a family meant a lot to both of them and so they found themselves, after much prayer and reflection, adopting first one daughter and then another because of their own difficulty in conceiving. As happens in so many cases (even though experts say that the statistics don't bear this out) they found themselves almost immediately giving birth to a son and then another. Suddenly they were a family of six with four children under the age of eight. Priorities had to change. Evaluation became necessary. Full-time teaching became C.C.D. teaching. Being an attorney became the means of buying a large enough home and providing for the growing family. School board involvement and pre-Cana weekends could not be as deep or frequent. Fortunately they both have enough confidence and faith in themselves and each other to know that as their children grow they will have the flexibility to reset priorities often and correctly. They are still exhausted. But they are at peace and they are doing well.

If there is to be enough time to love those we are called to serve, we must actively work to alleviate and dispose of those factors that rob us of the attention and energies needed whenever it is possible to do so. The Eucharistic minister who begs out of an evening of reflection on her own role because her mother has just been hospitalized is certainly making the right choice. On the other hand the one who chooses not to attend because, for whatever reason, he does not like the coordinator of Eucharistic ministers is not.

It must be noted that if we really love those to whom and with whom we are called to serve, time becomes less of a burden. We control it rather than it controlling us. After a welcome party for new parishioners on a Sunday evening, the lay organizers and the other parish staff members who worked the party ordered some pizzas, evaluated the evening, and finished the wine that had not been drunk by the guests. Everyone had to work the next day. But no one minded the enjoyment of each other and in basking in the success of the evening.

Far from being an enemy, time can and should be our ally. If we find that there isn't enough time to be serving all the people who need us, then perhaps we need to step back and see if we should even be there. Could it be that we are too selfish or too proud, feeling as if we're the only ones who can do it? Ministry means empowering others to join with us and we must never forget that. The warm, inviting, prepared lector will, by doing her job well, be encouraging others to join her in proclaiming the Word of God. She need not be the only lector at every liturgy.

Now that we've looked briefly at what it means to love those to whom we minister and how to try to find enough time to do it, we need to look at how we communicate that genuine love to them.

Throughout college I had the reputation of being the class jokester. Like any truly successful class clown, I learned early on the art of selecting only those classes where the professors would allow me the freedom to perform. In my own mind, I was a tremendous success in Doc Kelly's class. He was always laughing at my comments and antics. So it is not hard to imagine my surprise when another teacher took me aside and warned me that Doc was really upset with me. It seemed that I was the only one of the students that wasn't aware of the fact that he had suffered a stroke a few years earlier that left the muscles of his face affected. When he was angry he would appear to smile involuntarily and when he was really upset he would seem to laugh. And I was making him guffaw every class. Talk about miscommunication and not being able to read a person. Needless to say I decided to tone down so that I could survive the class.

How we communicate what we are feeling begins quite simply with how others view us. First impressions are based strictly on externals. And we need to be aware and cautious of that fact. I have had parishioners ask me why a particular Eucharistic minister never smiles, or shows any emotion at all when she's on the altar. A brief smile, a word to her family as they come up for Communion, a warm handshake of peace—there are so many little ways to communicate the caring attitude this person really has. Standing in front of church one particular Saturday evening and greeting people before Mass, I was mentally distracted by a meeting I had to attend later. A parishioner entering church looked at me and asked what it was I was so angry about. I wasn't angry at all. But then again I wasn't smiling and exchanging pleasantries either. How others see us, whether they are right or wrong in their perceptions, is important. We can't always control their poor judgment in reading us, but we can and should be aware of the cues we are sending out.

If the cliche "the eyes are the windows to the soul" holds any truth at all, then, obviously, eye contact is important in reaching out and touching others. It communicates not only attention, but also that a genuine connection has been made. Our eyes are the first communicators of the love that we have in us to share. As a priest I greatly prefer celebrating the Sacrament of Reconciliation face to face rather than in a confessional because of the eye to eye contact that can be made.

DO YOU LOVE ME?

Anyone who has ever tried to comfort or console someone over the phone knows the frustration of not being able to ''read'' the other person easily. How often do we find ourselves saying to the person on the other end of the phone that it would be better for him or her if we sat down together and talked?

But ''the look of love'' is certainly not enough. Think about it. How easy it is for many people to go through an entire day without being touched warmly by anyone. We are in a unique position to literally reach out to others with a gentle, non-threatening intimacy. Those who visit hospitals and nursing homes and shut-ins have the opportunity to communicate their love through a simple touch, a held hand, a shared embrace. The lonely often never feel the touch of someone who cares for them. When they are able, they substitute visits to doctors, barbers, or hairdressers in an attempt to feel someone's hands on them. This leaves us who are sensitive to this need with a tremendous opportunity and a tremendous responsibility. A wise pastoral associate selected as one of her goals to work her way through the senior citizens club of her parish, each month making some sort of physical contact with at least half of those in attendance. A firm handshake, a gentle pat on the back, a welcoming embrace, a helpful arm around a shoulder, a soft kiss on a cheek. Their response to her was obvious. They were never more animated and positive than when she was present. Now that's ministry, that's Christianity at work.

In fact, there are times that the only way we can communicate is to hold someone in silence. This is especially true at wakes and at other times of great sorrow. But it can be at joyful moments as well. How long did Elizabeth and Mary embrace silently before beautiful words were spoken? Words may not be there, but we are. And the love that we share as part of our ministry is communicated.

It is a shame that we who profess to care about others have often moved away from using touch as one of our tools. Touch can be there in every sacramental encounter, from the deacon who kisses the baby's forehead after pouring the baptismal waters, to the Eucharist minister who, after sharing the Body of Christ with a father, pauses to touch the child in his arms with a brief blessing. It can be there in every human encounter. It is healthy. It is proper. It is real. We need not, should not, run from it in fear.

Finally, and most obviously, we communicate our love with the words and prayers we share with others. We need to tell people they are loved whenever the opportunities arise. Words of encouragement, support, thanks and love are both appreciated and necessary. They can be scheduled and prepared or blurted out spontaneously. Scheduled in all of our parish pastoral council meetings is a ten minute go-around evaluation of the meeting. After one particularly frustrating meeting, where I felt very little had been accomplished, my own grumpy comments were terse and a bit authoritarian. However, when it was her turn, the seventy-five-year-old representative from the Altar Society smiled and said that she was especially pleased that the younger parishioners were taking such an active interest in the parish. Next to her sat the representative of the newly formed Sports Committee, a young father, under thirty years of age. He thanked the life-long parishioners for preserving such a beautiful parish,

DO YOU LOVE ME?

welcoming the new families in, and being people willing to be involved. He then spontaneously reached over and hugged the pleasantly surprised Altar Society representative. What a special moment. What real love was communicated.

Don't laugh. Ministry by mail is also an effective way to communicate care and concern. Most of us receive very little personal mail amid all the bills and fliers that are delivered to our door. A genuine note of thanks, an unexpected letter of appreciation, a thoughtful expression of concern, a clear vote of support—there are many ways to communicate the love we have. It's only a matter of taking the time to do it.

Our appearance, our eyes, our touch, our words all can help us to communicate the love we have for the people whom we serve. However the love has to be there or all that we do is hollow and empty. Looks, gestures, touches and words are not and can never be substitutes for the care and love we have. Rather, they are the vehicles to be used to show that love. Conversely they also allow others to show and express their love for us. And all of us know that a little love given in return goes a long way in restoring and rejuvenating our spirits and our willingness to keep on with our work.

What has been suggested here for us to do with the people we serve should also be done among the ministry staff as well. Opening ourselves to love cannot be turned on and off like a faucet. If there is little love expressed and exchanged at a staff meeting at 11:00 AM we cannot expect to have a great deal of love in us to share at a hospital visit at 1:00 PM. It just won't be there.

When Jesus asked Peter, "Do you love me?" and after Peter said that he did, the only advice Jesus gave him was

Dominic Grassi

"Feed my sheep." In other words, Peter, if you love me, show them you love them. But Peter, having recently denied Jesus three times certainly couldn't be feeling very good about himself. We cannot show others that we love them, we cannot express love to them unless we feel good about ourselves and love ourselves. Observing a teacher giving a talk to a group of high school students on retreat, I was struck not only by the inappropriate revelations about himself, but also how little self-esteem he had. The revelations did nothing but make the students noticeably uncomfortable and distant from the teacher. It was clearly not the right time or place to be trying to work out his own problems.

Ministry is both a privilege and a challenge that all of us as Christians are called to. It can be exhausting and draining. But it can also be tremendously rewarding. Those who are committed to it should feel good about themselves and the work they are doing. It is a great responsibility to be involved on such deep levels in people's lives. But we are only human. If health or job or personal problems start eating away at us, best to take some time off, because we won't be effective anyway, and let others care for us. Once healed and a little more whole and loving ourselves again, we'll be the better for it.

We must try to respond to Jesus' question "Do you love me?" during every encounter we have with the people of God. The more positive the response, not only in word but in action, the more genuine our ministry will be.

CHAPTER 2

"Lord, are you going to wash my feet?"

To serve or to be served

LIKE most young people starting out in adult public
life, as a newly ordained priest I was filled with what
could only be called a fiery altruism. Among the many goals
and standards that I had set for myself was that I would never
use my Roman collar to get any privileges. I felt, and rightly
so, that just because I was a priest I was not entitled to special
treatment. Well, when push came to shove, my passionate
idealism dampened very quickly.

Driving back to the rectory on a wintery Saturday evening,
I found myself pulled over by the flashing blue lights of a
Chicago police car. I jumped out of my car and immediately
asked the officer what I had done wrong. He responded by
asking me for my license. So I asked him again. He informed
me that I had passed another car over railroad tracks. I informed him that I didn't know that such an action was ille-
gal. He assured me that, indeed, it was. At that point he pulled
out his book of tickets. That's when I panicked. I quickly
loosened my scarf, opened my coat, and loudly cleared my
throat so that he would look up and be able to notice my white
collar and black shirt. Looking surprised, as I hoped he
would, the officer asked me if I were a priest. And when
I told him with as much humility as I could muster that I
most certainly was, before I knew it, my license was back

in my hand and I was quickly driving home unticketed; but in all honesty, not feeling too good about what had happened. I was genuinely angry with myself. I had just done what I had said I would never do. I had sold out.

As I drove down the block where I lived, I noticed one of the neighborhood alcoholics leaning against the rectory garage door. What was I going to do now? If I pressed the garage door opener he would fall right over. So that wasn't an option. I thought about riding around the block a few times hoping that he'd be gone when I came back. But he looked like he was ready to pass out. So I made up my mind and decided to earn the privilege that I had been given by the fine Irish Catholic police officer just a few minutes earlier. So I pulled over, parked my car on the street, took my inebriated friend by the hand, walked him to his one-room apartment, pulled his coat and shoes off, and laid him on his filthy bed. Just before he fell into his muscatel-induced sleep, he looked at me and smiled, "You're a good priest. Most of you guys would have pushed me out of the way or yelled at me." Small comfort to someone still feeling guilty. But some comfort at least.

A glance at the contents page of this book will quickly show that this chapter's title is the only question among those listed not asked by Jesus. It belongs to Peter, the disciple given a new name and set apart to lead the others; the one always at Jesus' side; the one whose nets were filled to bursting by Jesus; the one who walked on water with Jesus; the one who saw Jesus transfigured. If anyone should have understood what Jesus was trying to tell the disciples when he bent over to wash their feet at the Last Supper, Peter should have. But true to character, he did not.

These days, most of us in ministry aren't doing much better than poor old Simon Peter. Let's face it, most of us like our perks. We like the places of honor at banquets. We secretly enjoy the plaques and testimonials that we receive. And if people don't notice often enough, we find ways of letting them know how exhausted we are from all the hard work that we are doing so that they will have an opportunity to tell us how much they really do appreciate us. But that doesn't always work. A mother with two young children expressed her anger to a priest who was excusing himself early from a parish anniversary planning meeting because he "had the early mass tomorrow," by gently reminding him that she would be getting up earlier than he to feed her children and get ready for work herself.

And while this problem of expecting special attention has certainly been part of the growing disillusionment many people feel toward some priests, it is a temptation, if given in to, that can bring down the effectiveness of anyone who is trying to help others. The work is hard. There is a feeling that there isn't much recognition. And certainly all too often there isn't enough remuneration. We have to receive gratification where and when we can and so we start to grow soft on ourselves. The Director of Religious Education who enjoys treating the parish secretary like an indentured servant, the deacon who expects a free car wash at the teen club's fundraiser, the pastoral associate who always demands free tickets not only for himself but also for his entire family for every parish function are right up there with the pastor who would walk into the barbershop and not expect to wait his turn or pay for his haircut. At first glance there seems nothing too seriously wrong with what has just been described. The trouble sets in when such recognition becomes expected rather than a gift humbly accepted as a sign of gratitude.

Extreme examples? Possibly they are. Judgmental? Certainly, to some extent. But this should help to point out how the cancer can spread if it's not dealt with and how the work we do can be turned inside out completely. Usually the problem develops more subtly. But it is no less deadly. When the phone's ringing becomes an intrusion into our privacy rather than a welcomed call for our services, when hours put in are counted as more important than the insights shared and the hearts touched, it is when these things start to happen that we begin to slowly shift from serving others to expecting to be served. When our conversations become gripe sessions centering on what ludicrous demands people are now placing on us we are surely pushing ourselves above those we are expected to help, and that leads to our expecting them to defer to us in some way.

When our ministry turns into a job in our mind and is no longer felt or perceived by us as a vocation to which we have been called, we can find ourselves looking for more and varied compensation. And that can destroy our effectiveness. A religious who is a famous author and an acclaimed speaker, giving a presentation on the future of ministry in the church insisted on being picked up at the airport—a taxi was not acceptable. She was to be driven to one of the approved hotels on her list before being taken to the site of her presentation.

DO YOU LOVE ME?

There the chairs were to be set up in a particular configuration; water with lemon wedges and no ice was to be available to her on the podium and no cameras or tape recorders allowed. She certainly was saying something loud and clear about her vision of her work. Just ask any of the organizers who were on pins and needles until she, with a hefty stipend in hand, was on her flight out of town.

When the need to be served grows as important to us as the call to serve others, competition inevitably will set in with the others with whom we minister. We begin to look at what they have—a bigger office, a private phone, their name listed in the bulletin, their being selected to participate in Midnight Mass, even their being recognized by more parishioners—and we naturally want more for ourselves. Without much effort, a new hierarchy has been born, and, worse, so has a new clericalism.

There is no little irony when, at a staff meeting, the deacon sits with his deacon's cross prominently displayed on his chest and is called "deacon" by everyone in attendance while the pastor sits there in his golf shirt and is addressed as "Bob" by some and "Father" by others. And lest too pretty a picture is painted, the poor pastoral associate is referred to merely as "she" or "her" by both of the men. Confusing? Think about how their parishioners must feel?

Clericalism is not just represented by clothes that are worn or titles that are used, though these things often do reflect it and promote it. More certainly, clericalism is that attitude that says in so many ways that I am different than you. I am choosing to serve you and you are expected to be grateful. In fact, in some ways I am better than you, above you. And

37

while this is never verbalized, it does get communicated. Clericalism also can never be separated from a paternalism that lets people know that they have a place and they had better stay in it for their own good.

Where is the love that we must have for people in all of this? It is nowhere to be found. And people respond at best with a distant sort of respect and almost ceremonial deference. Or, at worst, some drift away from us and from the church while others actively and angrily choose to leave it.

Difficulties can also arise when people set us up on pedestals for whatever reasons. It's a natural tendency. Remember, there were times when the people wanted to crown Jesus as king. We need to find ways to break down this attitude and educate our people so that they will be comfortable in allowing us to minister to them. A priest working in an Hispanic parish responds to the elderly ladies who take his hands and kiss them as a sign of respect by taking their hands and kissing them in return. A small gesture, but significant. When is the last time anyone can remember seeing a bishop or cardinal return that same gesture?

A grammer school principal comes in to school about one Saturday a month to catch up on her paperwork. But she never fails to bring breakfast for the family who, week in and week out, clean the halls and classrooms and bathrooms in turn for a reduction in their tuition. She takes the time to eat with them and then she grabs a mop and helps them finish up. She starts her own work only when their cleaning is finished. She doesn't feel the need to tell anyone on the staff that she chooses to do this and she doesn't expect it of anyone else.

DO YOU LOVE ME?

Actions like these can challenge all to evaluate their relationships with those they serve.

Perhaps most damaging to those who start out helping others are those times, when for whatever reason, they are bitten by the advancement bug. It is no surprise that this can and does happen. Even the disciples argued as to who would sit at Jesus' right hand. And so it happens among us.

The musician who looks too longingly at a neighboring parish with a much larger music budget, a louder organ, a more professional choir, bigger congregation in attendance at Mass, and a better pay check for the one who directs it all, will find it harder, if not impossible, to love those with whom and for whom he or she currently works. The seminary rector who begins to believe all the rumors that he is hearing about his being in line to become a bishop loses the spontaneity, the edge, the creativity, and ultimately the humanity that made him such a well respected priest to begin with. People become either potential stepping stones or possible land mines and are no longer treated with love but with caution. The volunteer who grows jealous of the deacon whose hospital visits are accepted as more "official" by the hospital staff and often by the patients themselves, loses sight of the unique contribution her presence as an "ordinary" parishioner and neighbor can have, especially in calming people's fears. All of this goes back to being satisfied with ourselves, comfortable with ourselves, and able to love ourselves. We are then free to love the people to whom we minister and we are comfortable with the work we are doing. There is no need for any special recognition.

Dominic Grassi

There are many sad examples of people with tremendous talent and ability who, for whatever reasons, are always looking for something better. It is as if what they were doing was never good enough and so they must always be looking over their shoulders feeling as if they might be passed by.

Certainly all those who work with people need to be open to new avenues and ways of doing their jobs. And all of us need to be open to the new ministries that are being developed all around us. But we should also be comfortable enough with ourselves so as not to be threatened by all that is happening around us. This does not mean that people's roles won't change. They will and they should, especially when the change will bring about real growth and will help them to serve people better. This is different than either hardening ourselves to protect what we're doing because we are afraid of change or just riding the winds of whatever is the current thing to be doing.

How can we honestly determine if our motives in ministry are what they should be? The bottom line that determines if we are serving the needs of people is if we can say, like St. Paul said to the Corinthians, that it is Jesus that we preach and not ourselves. And how can we tell if this is what, in fact, is taking place? First of all, we need to listen to and to watch ourselves so that we might be able to evaluate ourselves honestly. Secondly, we need to listen to each other, to watch each other, and to be open to suggestions and evaluation by those with whom we share our work.

Thirdly, we need to be honest with ourselves. We need to look at our lifestyles, what is motivating us, the quality of our performance, at everything that affects or is part of our ministry. That is why it is essential for us to step back from our work to make retreats and to take vacations, even sabbaticals. We must remember that people need healthy and effective and whole people and that means taking time away from the job.

The pastor who won't allow parishioners into his living quarters for fear that they might think that he spends too much of the parish's money on decorating needs to be able to answer that concern honestly to himself, so that he will ultimately be able to be comfortable with his rooms. Hiding them from people is not an acceptable solution.

The director of religious education whose opening comments and welcoming of a guest speaker at a parish adult education program go longer than the allotted time given to the main speech needs to ask herself honestly why she needs to spend so much time at the podium. There certainly may be a valid reason for it. Perhaps she needs to set the stage for and support someone who some of the parishioners in attendance have found controversial. Then again, maybe her reasons are not so clear. Maybe she is just upset because she feels she could give a better talk on that topic than the speaker she's introducing. Only she can determine her real motivation. And she will be able to do that only if she is willing to take an honest look at herself.

Also, we need feedback from others, especially those with whom we minister. In a prayerful setting, homilies can be discussed and evaluated as can presentations to parents or letters sent to parishioners. Lectors can give feedback to each other as can those who take care of hospitality. Obviously there must be a level of trust and affection present if this is going to work. Staff meetings, scheduled evaluation sessions for particular people who share common tasks, prayer evenings—there are a limitless number of formats that allow us to share feedback with each other. A newly ordained deacon at a staff meeting, for example, discussed the homily he was going to preach at the first wedding that he was called upon to witness. He needed, in a gentle and nonthreatening way, to be told that what he wanted to say included too much about his joy and excitement at being a deacon and too little about the couple and the joy and excitement of their marriage.

No one in ministry is perfect. Each one of us regularly needs to be brought back to our goals and calling when we stray from them and start to be more concerned about our own needs for their own sake. Loving the people of God whom we serve is often difficult. We are human and we falter. It is at these times that we grow more self-centered and concerned about ourselves. We need to keep before us Jesus' example of washing the feet of his disciples. It needs to be an image that colors all we do for others. And Peter's questioning of Jesus' actions should serve as a reminder to us never to grow complacent or become self-satisfied. The call to involve ourselves in the lives of others, once it is accepted by us, means making the commitment to be the best ministers that we can be. And that means to love people before anything else. They deserve no less from us.

CHAPTER 3

"How does this concern of yours involve me?"

You are called to serve

WHEN I first saw them sitting in church, they were very noticeable. He came to well over six feet tall and she was under five feet, and pregnant. She looked very happy to be in church. On the other hand, he seemed only to be putting in time—probably for her sake. I later found out that they had just bought a sturdy old brick house a block from the church and were in the process of having it rehabbed. He worked downtown in the Commodities Exchange and she had been a nurse. Over the next few weeks I realized clearly almost all the enthusiasm for church was hers. But he did have an interest in basketball, and the parish just happened to be starting a Sports Committee that would be making decisions on how to make the facility usable and available both indoors and out for the school children and for the larger community. That became their tenuous call to become involved in the parish. With her encouragement, he joined the committee hoping that he would have a place close to home where he could play basketball after work.

Six months later, after a Sports Committee meeting, he took me aside and told me that initially he thought he would get reinterested in church when he finished college. But that, he admitted, didn't happen. Then he thought it would be when he got married. But it didn't happen then, either. Later he thought it would be for sure when his daughter was born and baptized. That didn't prove to be the case, either. It was at this point that he informed me that getting involved with the Sports Committee and, through that, feeling a part of the parish, that brought him back to the church—much to his own surprise.

Now, after a year's time, he has become one of the founding members of the Parish Pastoral Council. He is also taking a leadership role in a parish development program. As part of the Sports Committee, he helped plan and execute a major sports banquet. He has refereed grammar school basketball games. And he will be teaching sex education to the junior high students in the parish school. His wife has become a weekly volunteer school nurse and has given a talk to the school's Parent's Club. They both enjoy attending Mass and are well known in the parish. Ironically, as yet, he has not found the time to play a full game of basketball on the courts that he helped to repair. I don't think he minds that fact at all.

God calls us in the most unexpected ways to serve, to be Christian to others. That fact should be no surprise to us. After all, Jesus' first public act of ministry was nothing that would be considered very heroic. People at a wedding had drunk too much, too quickly, a common happening. The wine was gone and the host was embarrassed. Jesus' compassionate mother asked him to do something about it. And so, because of his intervention, jars that had been filled with water became jars filled with sweet tasting wine. The party was able to continue, much to the host's relief. Not too auspicious a begin-

DO YOU LOVE ME?

ning was this first miracle. But Jesus' work had to start somewhere. And, don't we all?

If you ask someone who is involved in the work of the church how they were called to it, how they got their start, more often than not the question will take them by surprise. It's hard to pinpoint one moment, one thought, one event, or one decision. For most of us, the call to serve others has been an ongoing and integral part of our lives. While some of us may have slipped into ministry quite naturally, others have fought it, tried to do other things, only to be hounded and brought back again and again to it. A classmate of mine, now an auxiliary bishop, decided way back in the sixth grade that he wanted to be a priest. The problem was that neither he nor anyone in his family were Catholic at that time! The priest who baptized him felt that it was either the biggest scam that he had run into in all his years of ministry or that this eager young man was really going to go places in the church.

For another person the word was not so easy nor the path so clear. Serious illness and other life crises had separated her from church but not from her idealism and working with people in the field of social work and community development. Salary was not important to her. So just as she was being forced to move out of her neighborhood because of higher rents, she stumbled onto a connection with a church with which she had not previously had many dealings. She found herself returning to it even though she had moved away. But she still feared involving herself too much. Initially she could handle being in the choir, and not much more. But strange things began to happen all at once in her life. Her

45

own job working with the disenfranchised in the neighbor-hood disappeared just as the parish started a Community Service Committee. With her background and experience, she was invited to chair it. And out of that commitment on her part has developed a growing ministry to the varied population of the parish and a growing sense of comfort with the church. She admits to not fully understanding how all this has happened to her.

If people just wait around for some magical call to fill their hearts with a burning ardor to serve others and for that call to spell out exactly what their work will be, they will be waiting for a long time.

The call to ministry which we are always free to accept or to reject comes to us, when, in the midst of what we are already doing, we notice something or someone who needs our help in some way. At that point we find ourselves not only asking the same question that was Jesus's, "How does this concern of yours involve me?", but we also find ourselves coming up with an immediate answer to that question. And that answer involves us enough to take the risk to respond to the need we have perceived and, in love, to act on it.

Some of the best lectors are very nervous when it comes time to walk up to the microphone and face the congregation. At the same time, even as they wrestle with their fears, they know that proclaiming the Word of God is their gift in love given to the parish and its people. And so they want to do it.

Most clearly, then, the call to serve others is not one isolated moment in history. Rather, it becomes an ongoing

DO YOU LOVE ME?

process of listening for and saying yes to the call of God's Spirit by responding to the needs of those whose concerns confront us. The call is intimately caught up in our response to it. There is no single moment of "ordination" for anyone. All in ministry are called by a people and their needs to serve them. A priest is not a priest unless he has a people who call him and affirm him by allowing him to be priest to them. A minister of care can neither minister nor care unless there are people calling her and empowering her.

Unlike the problem of which came first, the chicken or the egg, clearly the call to ministry by the people of God must come before and be a reason for a person to make the consistent and constant choice to help others. This ongoing process of responding to others is what makes the call we receive truly sacramental in nature.

The implications of this in terms of seminary training and other ministry programs in the church is staggering. Is everyone who wants to be minister actually called to be one? Is all that is necessary an invitation from a pastor or a raised hand of a volunteer? Does everyone have the proper skills to do it or will the Lord provide what is necessary? Does passing the right academic courses or training sessions make one ready to represent the church in helping others. To answer all of these questions thoroughly would take a book in itself.

But an answer must be given to the above questions and in each case it is "no." Credentials and degrees may be important, but they cannot be the sole criteria. Desire and vision are important but in and of themselves they are not enough. In order to be effective with people, as has been pointed out, one needs to be called from a people. How can a people know someone well enough to call them forth if that person is far away being trained by people who themselves have never experienced the call? More and more people expect not only the training, but also the temperament, and not only the aptitude but also the spirituality that will allow a person to truly serve them. Unfortunately, in too many cases and this certainly remains the situation in the appointment of pastors and associate pastors, ministers are imposed upon a community. If they are good and sensitive and caring, it still takes valuable time and energy for the people to accept them and call them to touch their lives. If they are not, disaster can occur. How difficult it becomes when an outsider comes onto a staff or, in some cases is given the responsibility of pastoring, and is surrounded by people who have come from that community, who have loved the people there, and have been ordained by their friends and neighbors to serve that church and who know that church so well. Until we are willing to find a better way than the traditional Tridentine seminaries that still dominate the scene and the ministry training programs that sadly mirror them, these tensions will remain. I can hear the howls of protest now from those in ministry training. The training in and of itself may be necessary. It is how people get into the programs that is often suspect.

In too many cases the people involved in the selection of ministers, fail to screen them before their arrival or fail to allow them to earn their place as ministers. And so some are doomed to fail from the start. Certainly most priests are not selected by the parishes to which they are appointed. And, as well, many youth ministers are hired from the outside. In spite of it all, many do succeed.

DO YOU LOVE ME?

To answer the call to serve others, a person has to be healthy and whole. Certainly, we are all human, and certainly we bring our life experience to our work. And that means we carry both our strengths and our limitations with us. But, stating it bluntly, there is a difference between being a wounded healer and being someone trying to help others with their life's blood pouring out of gaping psychological, spiritual or emotional holes. We can use our own weaknesses to better understand and love those whom we serve. But if our problems are so serious, how can we help others when we not only cannot help ourselves but are also being beaten down by our own difficulties?

Ministry, like so many of the helping professions, attracts people who choose to use the power it affords and who crave its ability to control intimacy. If such needs go unchecked, we are left with more and more among us who fall into child abuse or who are involved in adultery or who are overcome by addictions because of their tremendous feelings of guilt. The newspaper headlines are filled with too many of these horror stories. And every story, either publicly revealed by the media or whispered about in the vestibule of the church, hurts the credibility and the ability of all among us who are trying to do our jobs well. Adding to the confusion, very often these cases involve those who otherwise appear to be functioning very well. So how can people decide who among us to trust?

When these kind of serious problems arise, they need to be confronted and dealt with immediately to protect innocent people from being hurt. If a person, having received treatment, is deemed capable of returning, fine. But, for that

49

person's sake and for others who could be hurt, strict pa-
rameters need to be set. The people must be protected at all
costs. The church doesn't owe anyone the right to be a minister. If the privilege to serve others has been seriously
abused, that privilege may need to be taken away. Nothing
can hurt people more than being mistreated by the one they
felt they could trust, the one who should have responded to
them with love.

Putting it plainly, there are those in ministry who, for whatever reasons, are not capable of loving others. And since
that love of those we serve is the core of what it means to involve ourselves in the lives of others, they never should have
taken on those responsibilities. But they did and so they only
continue to hurt themselves. Tragically, the potential to hurt
some among those they are called to serve is always present.

This is not the place to cite examples, no matter how
general. Those of us who love the privilege of ministering
to others would find them too painful. We know exactly what
is being communicated here. We have all been touched by
the scandal, grief, heartbreak, and long-term problems that
are the results of such situations. We do not judge our brothers
and sisters. In love we pray for them.

Sadly, many of these problems could have been prevented.
For all their elaborate evaluation procedures, training programs, ultimately those responsible are notorious for allowing people with severe problems to fall through the cracks.
People are eager to take on new roles in the church. They
volunteer their time and energies. And so those in authority
are often reticent to deny them the opportunity unless major
problems have surfaced. Too often they rely on their own

set of criteria without checking with those who have worked intimately with the ones being evaluated. And to pass that kind of life altering judgment is difficult. Difficult it is, but a necessary responsibility.

It may have taken two or three years in the seminary to surface and to be noticed, but unless the seminarian who is an adult child of an alcoholic parent and who is very often abusive of others is willing to work out the problems involved from his youth, then ordination should be put off or refused him. The bishop's hands, the oils, none of that will magically change the limitations of his personality. The tenured teacher who regularly comes to school with alcohol on his breath from the night before and who has to be driven home after embarrassing himself at faculty parties should be confronted. Treatment should be demanded for his own good and ultimately for the good of the children he teaches. If he refuses he has to be dismissed. The pastor or principal or school board are failing in their responsibility if they choose to look the other way.

These are hard words. And certainly there are exceptions, people who have reached inside themselves and with the help of others and of God have worked through very serious problems and are once again able to do wonderful, sensitive, caring work. But the deciding factor must be the well-being of those who are searching for help.

The call to minister to the people of God, as it comes in so many ways, through so many people and their needs, can be a source of genuine personal growth for all of us. But we need to do more than just hear the people who are extending the call to serve us. There must be something in us, in our ability to listen, in our wisdom and compassion and gentleness that has touched those who call to us. Something we have done allows people to know and to feel that they are loved by us. Conversely, we as ministers need to feel their love for us in return if we will be able to go on effectively. The Parish Pastoral Council that asks the temporary chairperson to continue on in that capacity indefinitely is not only saying that they admire his talent for running meetings in general and appreciate the work he did in preparation for that meeting in particular. They are also saying that they trust his fairness and evenhandedness in bringing them to decisions about the parish. And if they didn't care for him personally, they would not have unanimously chosen him as they did. He has every right to feel good about himself.

Initially, Jesus' response to his mother may have sounded callous and uncaring both toward her and toward the embarrassed party throwers. But Jesus' actions ultimately show the depth of his concern. He does respond to his mother's call. Her concerns and those of the hosts, became his. His love for his mother allowed him to share in her feelings for them and so it is in love that he is able to assist them.

In this chapter we have seen that if we are healthy we can, the same way as Jesus, be called by others. Whatever form our service takes, our response can only be to love those who call us to them. Certainly that is why we must be capable of loving freely and without conditions. But things don't always come that simply. And that is why the next topic to look at is what it means to minister to, and so to love, people we don't like or who don't respond to us or whom we cannot understand. It's not easy.

CHAPTER 4

"If you love those who love you, what right have you to claim any credit?"

How do you love people you don't like?

FROM the first day it was announced to the parish community that she had been hired to be a pastoral associate, she, as a nun, as a woman, and as a minister, was subjected to nothing but abuse from one of the parish's venerable "pillars." She could not avoid him. He was an elected member of the parish pastoral council, on its finance committee, a lector at Sunday liturgies, chairperson for the last ten years of the annual parish carnival, and what appeared to be most important, an occasional golf partner of the pastor. He was around the rectory and the church as often as the housekeeper, and she lived there—or so it seemed to the pastoral associate.

Being semi-retired, the man had plenty of time on his hands. He was well liked and respected by many parishioners. So at first the nun thought that her reaction to his comments was brought on by her being a little oversensitive and insecure in her new job. But more and more, she began to feel that what he was saying was too often pointed and hurtful. She even found his quiet wife shaking her head in embarrassment as if she were apologizing for him.

He was subtle at first, always polite and never without a smile on his face. Often times he would appear not to be speaking to her, but, he still, of course, wanted her to hear every word.

It began the day they were introduced. He looked her up and down and then remarked that nuns who wore habits were the real powers in a parish. She did not wear a habit. He always spoke down to her and called her "young lady," his reason being that it was too hard to call someone sister who wasn't wearing a veil. At finance committee meetings, even when she presented a proposal, his questions were always directed to the pastor. Once at a parish party, still smiling, he suggested that she belonged in the kitchen with the rest of the women who were preparing the food. A major cause of pain was when she overheard him talking to his cronies about the need to tighten the parish budget. It was his feeling that if a nun wasn't willing to work merely for room and board in the convent, then she was a luxury that the parish couldn't afford. At that moment she consciously walked into his line of vision and he raised his glass in a mocking toast to her.

A week later he was hospitalized with phlebitis. She was the first of the parish staff to visit him since it was the pastor's day off and he had found an available golf partner. She brought him Holy Communion that day and every day he was hospitalized. She also brought flowers and a signed card from the rectory staff, cookies she baked that he wasn't supposed to eat, and a sympathetic ear with which to listen to his fears about being hospitalized. At daily Mass, at the Intentions she prayed for his return to health. When the pastor expressed his surprise by telling her, as if she didn't already know it, that she was praying for someone who wasn't among

DO YOU LOVE ME?

her biggest supporters, she smiled and told him that she knew that. What she didn't tell him was that her prayers for his return to health did not include that it needed to happen in the near future. But in reality she was able to see a different man lying there in bed. She sensed after his return to health that his comments had softened a bit. Or perhaps, she, at least, found herself less offended by them.

Would they eventually grow to be friends? That's doubtful. Would she ever really like him? It's highly unlikely that she would or that he would even let her. But minister to him, love him, in his time of crisis, this she was able to do well. She worked hard at it, almost as though she needed to prove a point to him as well as to herself.

Those who are genuinely called to an active role in the church today have a capacity to love that they are able to communicate almost unconsciously to others. It is what eventually binds people to them. It invites people to take the risk and to open themselves up to the love that the minister has for them. But beyond all else, the love that is offered to others is free to be accepted or rejected by them. If we genuinely care about people, but they choose not to respond and, therefore, do not allow us to enter their lives, that can be very painful to any one of us who has reached out.

Most of us have experienced such pain. More often than not, we respond by allowing ourselves time to pause in order to reevaluate both our motives and our techniques. We may even choose to try again. But if, when all is said and done, we have given it our best shot and our offer to reach out to others is rejected, we should be able to accept that reality and move away. Perhaps we will back off entirely from that situation. Or perhaps we might attempt to pursue a friendship relationship rather than a ministerial one.

None of us likes rejection, especially when our motives are good. We think about the disciples who were told to shake the dust from their feet and to move on. And we try our best to do the same. It is at times like these that we find ourselves rightly turning to those who really care about us for the affirmation that we need. We find ourselves praying a bit more, as well. And so, we survive, and, chances are, the person whom we attempted to reach will survive as well, with the grace of God, or perhaps, with someone else being the helper who was needed.

All this is difficult enough. But it is nothing compared to the ones who, for whatever reasons, find themselves in situations where they are called upon to minister to someone that they find very hard to like, much less to love. As in the pastoral associate's story we've just encountered, it may be because the very person who we are expected to care about and help is either rejecting us or hurting us in some way.

At other times it may not be that black and white. Sometimes no matter how hard we try, no matter what methods we use, there are people we just can't seem to like, either over the long haul or in a brief encounter.

The parish social worker is having a bad day. The last thing she needs is grief from the street person to whom she has handed a sandwich at the door of the rectory. He complains to her, that there is no meat in it. She explains, almost apologetically, while listening to her unanswered phone ringing, that peanut butter and jelly was all that was left. He throws the sandwich at her feet in anger. He calls her a

number of colorful names, the least offensive of which is
"fool." Her patience has now disappeared. Stung by his
words, she picks up the sandwich, telling him that he's the
real fool because he is going to go hungry. She hears the
spite in her own words, is sorry, and quickly softens. She
calls out a blessing to the poor soul as he starts down the
stairs. He stops, turns back, and shouts in her face that God's
a fool too. This gives her the first reason to smile that day.
She looks at him gently and says that if that's the case, it
put them both in good company. She holds out the sandwich
again and he takes it without saying another word.

There is that almost compelling notion that those involved
in caring professions must treat everyone who comes to the
door or into his or her life as a potential Jesus. This certainly has some validity. Jesus himself challenges us. He tells
us in no uncertain terms that we cannot claim any credit,
we cannot really call ourselves Christians, if the only people
with whom we are willing to share love are those whom we
know well or who have already shown us love. The challenge is to find the image and presence of God in those whom
we do not like. It is at that moment, in what is sometimes
nothing more than an unguarded instant of intimacy, that we
can see what in that person is limiting us or what in ourselves
is holding us back. That is enough, sometimes, to make connection. Perhaps what happens is that we see a bit of ourselves
and our weakness in that person. Whatever the dynamic, it
becomes enough to allow us to be the person needed in that
situation.

An engaged couple who somehow had missed two marriage preparation sessions without calling the priests, lost the

booklet needed to plan their ceremony, and came forty-five minutes late for their rehearsal, finally showed up for their wedding with blood tests, but no license. The groom thought that the test papers were all he needed even though the priest specifically asked him to bring the license to the rehearsal the night before, which he didn't do. It's not hard to see why the priest had grown to dislike the couple. Now there was no license and so he was ready to go through the church roof. He was tempted to chase all twenty members of the bridal party and the two hundred guests out of church, turn off the lights and lock the doors. But one look at the poor bride in her dress holding a swiftly wilting bouquet and crying reminded him how difficult this once-in-a-lifetime special moment had become for her. So the priest called a lawyer and other priests and found that there was no legal way to marry them without a license. It took a little creativity and compromise. They ended up having a somewhat extemporaneous liturgy to celebrate their love. While no vows were exchanged, pictures still were taken, rice was thrown, and a party held. It was the best that could be done given the circumstances. The next week when the license was finally secured, he married them in a private ceremony with their families present.

Often times, we can overcome our difficulty in certain relationships by trying to understand the depth of the other's feelings during those crises or life-changing times when they need the church's care. This may still not be liked by the care giver, but he or she should be able to respond in love to what they are feeling so strongly. A heart to heart connection occurs.

This does not mean that we should pity people or look down

on them because of their problems or because of what they are feeling. That would be counter-productive and patronizing. Rather it means to genuinely feel with or be empathetic with them. It is their feelings rather than who they are that can call out to and connect with us.

We have to be honest with ourselves and constantly monitor our feelings about others. If we do not realize that we dislike someone, or if that feeling starts slowly and then begins to grow and we are not aware of it, we might find strange things happening to us. For example, we might find ourselves becoming frighteningly legalistic. The deacon decides that he will not baptize a couple's baby because they were not registered in the parish. Whereas the week before he may have used a similar request to invite a couple he liked to register after he had performed the baptism. The C.C.D. teacher insists on seeing the parents of an uncooperative child, threatening to hold back Confirmation, while at the same time, other students have missed more classes and done fewer assignments than this disliked child.

Something else may happen. We may go through the motions with none of the spirit, the heart, or the soul involved in each service. The minister of care may spend the same amount of time with the shut-in that she really doesn't like because of his complaining as she does with others she visits. But her thoughts are not with the person and neither is her heart. Her visits have far less impact than they should. And she may not even be aware of it.

If there's someone in a position of ministry who really doesn't like people at all, it is obvious that these problems will multiply. They may give themselves any of a number of titles, but they are the ones who hide behind Canon Law, parish rules and regulations, their own personal standards, anything that keeps them from interacting on a loving level with people. And when their position forces them to act with genuine care, these in-name only ministers do nothing more than go through the motions with no feelings at all.

It also must be noted that anyone who is so much in love with himself or herself will not be capable of loving others. People will never measure up to this minister's standards. There will always be something to find fault with. This self-love blocks all ability to genuinely care about others. And because they feel looked down upon, people cannot reach out to the minister. That self-love can be found in the minister's attitude about himself or his abilities, or it can be found in an overpowering preoccupation with possessions. We have all heard stories about a priest too busy washing his car to see someone who came to the rectory with a problem but not an appointment.

Conversely, those who attempt to be of service to others but are unable to love themselves are also incapable of loving others. They might succeed in creating an unhealthy, co-dependency relationship with someone. Or they might develop some kind of self-destructive addiction. But they will never love or be loved.

At times the problem goes beyond ministers disliking one person or another. The problem is not their attitudes about themselves either. What develops centers on the understanding of others or the lack of it. Because we are not comfortable with or are unable to understand a particular culture or perhaps do not have a handle on our own prejudices, we

DO YOU LOVE ME?

are not able to connect with people, answer their call, and in love serve them as they deserve.

No one should have to feel locked into a position of service in which they are uncomfortable. Nor should they be expected to stay with people with whom they do not feel comfortable. There must be other options available. For example, in a racially changing parish, we can choose to learn more about a particular culture or ethnic group in order to grow closer to a people. The first thing a principal of a grammar school in one such parish did upon returning from a summer institute on African-American culture was to drop ''My Little White Guest'' as the song sung by the second graders at their First Communion Mass. The second thing she did was to make the commitment to spend an evening with every family from the parish that had children registered in the school. Through her efforts to reach out and to listen and learn, the school stabilized and in its own way prospered. The principal herself felt less besieged and more in control of the school. Most importantly, she became recognized as a person who cared about all the children.

But those who find themselves in these difficult situations need to realize that one summer-school class in a particular language or a weekend seminar or study group on a particular ethnic group will never be enough to change attitudes or to create an understanding that isn't already there in some form. It takes more than those good but feeble efforts. Along with any kind of learning and studying, which is, of course, very important, there must also be a commitment to accept people for who they are and not to try to make them more like us in order to be able to more easily serve them. Such actions are not fair to them and really shouldn't be labeled as ministry. It's actually closer to coercion.

It was not until many years later that I realized what my sixth grade teacher had done. She had designated the first two rows of the classroom as "Sleepy Hollow" and therein she placed the students who had the darker skin or who spoke with accents. They were different. And she was determined, as she would proudly say, to make them like the rest of us. And she was doing it for their own good.

We will better represent the church if we realize and make a conscious effort to learn from people who are different from us and yet who still need serving in some way. There is such a richness that can be ours if we are willing to open ourselves up to them. We could learn so much.

All this points out our basic limitations when we come from outside a community. In such cases, the ultimate service that we can provide for people is to break down what has become the "Plantation Mentality" of trying to help outsiders knowing what is best for those who are different or who are lower on the economic scale, or who are recent arrivals, or whatever. We must be willing to empower them to call up their own leaders from their own ranks. In effect, we work to make the need for our presence with them obsolete. And this can only be done by genuinely loving them.

Special recognition needs to be given to those who choose to involve themselves in peoples' lives where rapid and often angry changes are taking place. It takes a heroic amount of love to reach out to very different people with their very separate agendas and needs and be able to serve them. There are very few supports built into such a calling. But the tremendous potential for healing is there, as is the opportunity to uphold and reaffirm the just and right position of the Gospel to all the people.

The final point that needs to be made here is that no one should ever feel "locked in" or trapped in ministry. If a person is having a problem with a particular parishioner and is not able to find a way of loving that person, there is nothing wrong with admitting that the opportunity for helping is not present there. That person can either find someone else to be the minister in that situation or simply tell that individual that he must find someone else. The pastoral associate who has heard too much about a husband and has already formed strong negative judgments of him (and so would not be an effective marriage counselor for the couple) can steer the couple to a more neutral source, either within the parish or elsewhere (and that is one reason we need to have good networks). Or the pastoral associate can decide to tell the couple that, quite frankly, because of what she already knows and because her feelings about the husband are already set, she would not be the one who could properly help them. Better that, either with her help or separately, they find someone else. Her honesty is not rejection of them but the best response she can give as a minister.

In the larger situation of not understanding or appreciating a different culture, race or ethnic group, the minister very much needs to know when it is time to move on for his or her own good and for the good of the people. With most of those in volunteer positions or parish staffs, this change happens naturally as they move on to another parish. People who remain tend to want to make things work out. If that doesn't happen due to forces greater than themselves, it is better for them to leave. It makes little sense to be a Eucharistic Minister at a Mass celebrated in a language you don't understand and with which you are not comfortable. Pastors and associates and others not tied to a parish by homes or families have more flexibility in this area. But they are cautioned to use it wisely. Neither running away or digging your heels in are conducive to effective ministry.

I am not advocating that either staying or leaving is the best response in these complex situations. All of us need to be honest with ourselves and need to decide how best we are able to love and therefore to serve the people of God. For some among us it will be by staying. For others it will mean moving on. In neither case is it advocated that people be abandoned. As church we are always obligated to offer alternatives to individuals and to allow those who are better able to either come in or rise up out of the community and do the job.

Through all these processes as we evaluate the many different relationships of which we are a part, we must be open to the Spirit. With prayer, that openness can allow for surprising moments of grace to occur in our lives. What may occur is that we may find ourselves ministering to those whom we love and who love us in return. But in strikingly different situations, to our credit, we may allow our loving God to work through us. And, after all, it is for him that we do all that we are called to do.

CHAPTER 5

"Has no one condemned you?"

You must love, to love is not to judge

I HAD been assigned to the parish, my first, for well over a year before she was brought to my attention. Crippled by arthritis and other ailments, she was no longer able to leave her small home. While her body may have been giving out, her mind was still strong and her memory was razor sharp. I found out about her through a former parishioner who had asked about her. She had been forgotten. So I called her and introduced myself and asked if she would like to have Communion brought to her. She was hesitant at first and then she finally agreed. I thought that I'd only be there for a short while, but we sat and talked for over an hour. She was delightful and filled with stories. When it came time for Communion, she asked if she could receive the Sacrament of Reconciliation first, not an unusual request. This warm and caring person told me a sad story. She had not been to Communion or Confession for over fifteen years. And she wanted to tell me why.

She had moved up to the city from the rural South with her very young children. She found an apartment for her family in a depressed ghetto neighborhood. She had been brought up a devout Baptist. But, as chance would have it, the apartment was directly across the street from the Catholic church.

She quickly became impressed by the warmth and the openness of the parishioners there as well as the priests and staff. All this finally led to her being baptized and welcomed into the Catholic Church. Not too much later an opportunity arose for her to move her family into a new house in a middle-class neighborhood undergoing racial change further south in the city.

She expected her new Catholic parish to be as welcoming and inviting as was her original one. It wasn't. She found herself and her children spit at on the way to church. The white ushers would seat them only in the very last pews of the church. After a few months of being treated so poorly she decided to talk to the pastor about what was happening. She made an appointment to see him. He did not invite her into his office, but rather stood in the doorway of the rectory talking with her. She told him honestly how it pained her to have her children spit at and how the ushers were mistreating her and her family. She expected the pastor to help her. Instead, red faced and indignant, he told her that she was an evil woman, a sinner for spreading such lies. And then he ordered her to go right into the church and ask the Lord to forgive the grievous sin she had just committed by talking to him that way. She told me that she left the steps of the rectory stunned. She had thought that all Catholics were open and compassionate like those she had first met in her original parish. She told me that she just couldn't obey the pastor and go to the church to pray like he had demanded that she do. And because she didn't obey him and because she couldn't bring herself to confess something that she felt in her heart was not wrong, she could not in good conscience continue to receive Holy Communion. And so it was that she stopped for fifteen years!

I invited her to receive the Eucharist again that day. But first I apologized to her for all the wrong, hurtful and judgmental words that the pastor had shouted at her those many years ago. I assured her that she had committed no sin. I tried to make it a moment of genuine reconciliation between her and a church that had rejected her for too long a period of time.

When we serve others it is crucial that we do not pass judgment upon them. Jesus never did. Yes, he did call the Pharisees "whited sepulchers" and worse. And yes, he did physically and verbally attack the money changers in the temple. And yes, he even condemned the entire city of Jerusalem. He was compelled to do so because he was also a prophet who saw the world clearly and knew those who would refuse to accept him. And so it was in justice that he spoke out against them, as we too are called to do. How to be both minister and prophet will be discussed in a later chapter.

Jesus ministered to the poor, to the social outcasts, to those who came to him without any hidden agendas, much to the surprise of his disciples and often to the dismay of the others who followed him around. The woman who had been caught in adultery had been condemned and judged. Jesus chose to break up the mob and minister to her. He selected a hated tax collector named Matthew to be one of his chosen disciples. He dined with the despised little Zaccheus, much to the scandal of the righteous. He invited the repentant thief who hung beside him on a cross into the Kingdom of Heaven. There are many more examples that could be given. It was the unloved and the unlovable to whom Jesus came. He chose to love them rather than to judge them. That must be the model we follow in his church today.

With all those examples in scripture, why then are we so ready and so quick to pass judgment on others? Are we blessed with some kind of special "second sight" that allows us to penetrate into the hearts and souls of people so that we can clearly see what their motives always are? I think not. Yet why is it that we are so quick to announce to a couple that because they do not attend mass weekly, we have decided that their faith is not strong enough to have their child baptized by us? Or, how is it that we are able to decide so easily that a particular group — teens or yuppies or Italians or whoever—aren't interested at all in the church so why should we bother to reach out to them?

As long as the church remains as hierarchical as it is rather than being the communal gathering of the people of God that it should be, it will succumb to the temptation of judging others. Hierarchical structures feed on those high up passing judgment or those below them, in order to justify their existence and to protect the structure and their place in it. When a cardinal from the Curia in Rome feels compelled to warn the American Church that women have soft hearts and are controlled by their emotions, is he doing anything more than attempting, albeit poorly, to protect the sagging structure of an ordained, male, celibate priesthood? Inevitably such feeble attempts cause massive alienation.

Some would argue that without the hierarchical structures in place, the Catholic Church would lose its universality and would become congregationalist in its outlook. There is a

DO YOU LOVE ME?

place for hierarchy if those who are a part of it see themselves as true servants of the people rather than as judges and protectors of the truth. The structures should exist to aid others in their work and to help accomplish on the larger scale the goals of the local communities.

This can only be accomplished if there is genuine care and love exhibited by those whose roles make them a part of that hierarchical structure. If this isn't the case, then there is no reason for those structures to be in place.

The bishop's secretary who tells someone who has asked for an appointment with the bishop that the earliest he can be seen by his eminence is in three months, and then cuts short any protest by saying that the bishop is a very busy man, is no better than the parish with the sign that reads office hours are from 9 to 12 on its rectory door. On the other hand, the Office of Evangelization whose staff spends most of their time in the parishes custom developing programs, listening, sharing resources, and helping staffs and other groups reach their full potential by taking people where they are, is doing the people of God a genuine service.

Similar hierarchical structures exist on the parish level as well. The iron-fisted pastor who tells the parish school faculty that he is the final arbiter of what will be taught in the religious education classes is passing judgment on people far better trained and often more capable than he. While such an example shows an obvious abuse of structures, there are times when structures can more subtly sneak up on us without our realizing it and block our contact and immediacy with people. This newly formed hierarchy can undo tremendous good that has been accomplished.

Dominic Grassi

A phenomenally successful parish grew from just a handful of families to thousands in only a few years largely due to the strength and the vision of its newly formed staff. The initial group involved in the work were very "hands on" and creative in their approaches. Everything was done with a personal touch. Not surprisingly, the people responded readily to them. But success brought with it growth and the growth brought the need for a larger staff (read, structure). And distance between the original ministers and the people grew. When the regular cantor at the Saturday evening Mass is asked a series of formal questions by a secretary whom he has never met, in order to have his child scheduled to be baptized and he never comes into contact with the staff member who had invited him and drawn him into the life of the parish initially, something terribly wrong has happened even though it would appear that the parish was functioning better than ever. The cantor, rightly or wrongly, was left with the impression that this secretary had the authority to pass judgment on him and on his child. And while she did indeed approve the baptism, after he convinced her he was Catholic, he has begun to actively look for another parish with a little more personal touch in which to involve himself.

In any parish, the most effective ministry is that which is personal and hands on. As parishes grow, so too must the number of those who are involved in its work. But ideally, each one needs to reflect the common vision of church that is the parish's. If even a few of those who are involved in its work are harsh, too business-like, or judgmental in their style and outlook, it can potentially color and possibly damage the parish's entire operation. No parish staff that has worked

70

so hard to make a parish succeed wants that to happen. But it can and it does.

The couple in charge of the Baptismal Preparation Program in a parish stumbled upon the fact that the Deacon, when asked by people to have their child baptized, asked all sorts of personal questions and made a number of demands that reflected his own personal theology but unfortunately were not part of the expressed policy of the parish staff in regard to baptisms. He was confronted and when he failed to change his position and his actions, the staff made it clear to him that he was not to deal with parishioners in this area. His task was to refer the parents to the couple in charge of the program and they would carry out the parish policy.

We can look at the larger church and we can look at the parish as the local church and see fairly easily how judging others is not what parish life is all about. So much takes place on a more intimate level, person to person, face to face. And it is at this point that those involved need to be extremely cautious in avoiding any semblance of passing judgment on others, especially when the good of the other person is not perceived to be the most important concern.

I received a telephone call from a very upset parishioner whose daughter, though not married, was pregnant. A good friend of hers from another parish, using a very obvious hierarchical structure to justify herself (she had announced that she was in the Lay Ministry Training Program) told the woman that her pastor, I, would have to refuse to baptize the baby after it was born because it was illegitimate. That was unsolicited information that was totally wrong and passed on very judgmentally. When I assured the parishioner that it was within my jurisdiction to baptize the baby and that I was pleased that her daughter had, first of all, chosen to bring the baby to term, and, secondly, to have the child baptized, it brought her the peace that had been snatched away from her by a so-called friend. Two weeks later, the same woman who had made all the false statements about what I could do called me. She not only identified herself as a candidate in the lay ministry program, but also as an officer in her parish's Right to Life Committee. I guess that she was trying to impress me with her credentials. She had called me because she felt that I should know that the young woman who was having the baby did not intend to marry the father. With that information, she was sure I would reconsider the baptism. Her voice was victorious, smug, and not a little judgmental. So in my anger, I pulled rank on her. In the sweetest voice I could muster, I reminded her that I was the minister in this situation and I would make the proper decision as I saw fit. She need not bother herself with it anymore. The baby was baptized. The family, including the mother of the baby, and the child are regular in their Mass attendance. The bottom line is that we are not called upon to be judges.

Sometimes people demand of us answers that are black and white. They want us to make the decisions that will keep them from having to make their own choices. They want us to tell them what is right and what is wrong, what they should be doing and what they should avoid. It's tempting to give them what they want. It's easy to give them the simple, textbook answers, pat them on the head very patronizingly, and send them on their way. It's not very difficult to make decisions for them, to make the judgments they don't want to make themselves.

But that is not what we are all about. It's just too easy. We must first help people to realize that they should come to their own decisions and conclusions about those concerns that directly affect their lives. It is too easy to ask for and to receive answers from others and to do what they tell us to do. Ultimately, such behavior is immature, and it is a cop-out. It robs people of their freedom. Once people are able to realize that they need to take control and to make their own decisions we must be committed to stay with them throughout the long and often difficult decision-making process. We are to support them, encourage them, challenge them, and once they have made their decision, whatever it may be, love them unconditionally. This process certainly takes much longer than handing out advice, but it is the only way to help people to grow and mature.

A young couple stayed around after a parish pre-Cana marriage preparation program. They wanted to talk to the married couple who, along with a priest, had been the team that presented the evening to the couples. Serious in-law problems had begun to surface even before the wedding. It was causing them great pain. What should they do? Rather than giving them five minutes of quick advice after a long and grueling day, the married couple chose to call their baby sitter and tell her that they would be later than expected. They took the engaged couple out for a pizza, listened to them, and helped them come to their own conclusions of what would be best for them to do. It was a three-hour process, followed in the weeks to come with some concerned phone calls. Rather than easily judging that the couple was immature or that the accused in-laws were overly protective, the married couple realized that as ministers they needed to help this young man and woman deal with their hurt and confusion so that they could formulate their own best response to their situation. What happened in this instance showed clearly the difference between judging others and ministering to them.

To minister to others without judging them takes many skills. But it also takes a great deal of humility. Our attempts to help others do not make us better or holier or wiser than anyone else. The most effective among us rather, know our own limitations and our own faults and failings. This realization of being no better or no worse than those to whom we serve allows us to better understand where others are coming from as they struggle with the problems and concerns of their lives. Compare the humble lector with the one who is all puffed up with himself/herself. Which one better proclaims the work of God? Scripture gives us the example of the Publican and the Pharisee to remind us that without humility, we cannot help ourselves, much less others.

Without humility we become pompous. We grow impatient. We are mere advice givers who are seldom sought out and even less often listened to. We grow blind to our own limitations. We then blame everyone else for our lack of success. The prayers we pray most often must be prayers of thanksgiving, prayers that thank God for working through us and allowing us with all our limitations to be effective.

It was only when Jesus pointed out to the crowd which

DO YOU LOVE ME?

was so eager to stone the woman caught in adultery that they too were sinners, that their righteous judgment evaporated into the dry desert air.

The stones they so willingly had picked up fell to the ground harmlessly and they wandered off lost in their own thoughts. Ready to defend the law moments earlier, they now were reflecting on their own faults. Jesus then turns his attention to the woman and gently asks, "Has no one condemned you?" That question remains for us a reminder that no one can be helped, no one can be healed if judgment is simply passed upon them. If we choose ministry, we choose to love and not to judge.

CHAPTER 6

"Would you betray me with a kiss?"

To serve when hurt and in pain

AT TWENTY-THREE years of age, the young man is earning well under fifteen thousand dollars a year, not even enough to afford an apartment for himself. He is teaching in a small, private school for behavior-disordered youths. He has come home from work with bruises and bite marks and has recently been treated in a hospital emergency room after a file cabinet was pulled down on top of him. He lives in a forgotten third-floor corner of a twenty-eight room rectory. In exchange for his room and board, he does some painting and, when he has the time, some work with the parishioners. After spending eight years of high school and college in a seminary system thinking about the priesthood, he found it necessary to take a break from it, but not completely. He is a natural with people, attentive to their signals and able to respond to them with amazing speed and accuracy. Consequently, a lot of people are easily attracted to him. And so, at this point in his life, he finds himself torn between finding a job that would give him the money and, as importantly, the freedom that his youth craves, and the satisfaction and good feeling that he gets from working with people. For some among us, a life of service comes naturally. He is one so blessed. And he knows it. That is part of his struggle.

DO YOU LOVE ME?

You would not know it to look at him now that he once possessed an extremely volatile and self-destructive temper that would flare up over the smallest of issues and then expand like a nuclear reaction destroying everything in its path. It was the kind of temper that would not only hurt all those around him, but was capable of really hurting him. It was a temper that was born out of an anger that he really could not express nor pinpoint. What he was not able to see, unfortunately, was clear and visible to many others around him. From a large family, he was a middle child, short in stature, created in the identical image of his father and also carrying the sensitivity of his mother. Both parents were alcoholics. Fortunately, the mother recognized her problem and was able to hold the family together by the very strength of her will. But there were many difficult times. It was only when he reached the last stages of high school that the family, with the help of a counselor, did an intervention with the father, a decent and good man who was finally able to admit his problems and to act on them.

From this description it is clear that this young man is a classic example of an adult child of alcoholic parents, a situation about which volumes have now been written. Fortunately, instead of his past tearing him down or limiting him in some way, he has been able to use the pain and the confusion, the hurt and the anger to forge for himself a personality and a temperament that make him natural with people. He has worked hard to control his temper and to understand what caused it. He is especially good with children and with young people. He is able to sense their hurts and, with his honesty, help them through their troubles. It would appear fairly certain that whatever his future holds, there will always be people who will be touched by him and his love and concern for them. He is a person who has more than just survived. He is one of life's winners.

One of the necessary qualities for a person to be effective in helping others is sensitivity. But sensitivity can be both a blessing and a curse. Certainly it can help us understand and feel what people are going through so that a loving response can be offered to them. On the other hand, the same sensitivity that can be so helpful can also leave us open to a tremendous amount of hurt. The choice appears to be either to desensitize ourselves and so risk becoming less effective, or accept the hurt and the greater risk of someday being ultimately overwhelmed and beaten down so that we can be as effective in loving and feeling with people as possible. How much do we want to gamble? How much faith in God's grace are we able to marshal?

Two very vivid and different situations come readily to my mind. A group of teachers went out for a pizza after a long evening chaperoning a high-school dance. Everyone was tired and hungry. Defenses were down. One of the teachers who had remained uncharacteristically quiet throughout the evening finally put her menu down and softly stated that her mother would have to undergo open-heart surgery. There was a moment of silence at the table. One of the priests seated at the table, a person who had a Ph.D. in Educational Psychology and years of experience teaching and counseling, looked up and asked if they wanted pepperoni on their pizza. So much for sensitivity. The pain of what she had shared, now somewhat muted, was picked up by someone else, rather self-consciously, but the damage had been done.

The second story is that of a parish secretary, a woman with no formal training in helping people, who chooses to take half of a morning to schedule First Friday Communion calls. When she makes the calls, she takes time to listen to the concerns and the fears of the elderly. Most of the time she just lets them talk. Next to their name and visitation time she leaves any note or comment that may be helpful for the minister bringing the person the Eucharist. Birthdays get remembered and doctors reports are asked about. A busy person with a lot of other responsibilities, the secretary takes the time to show a real sensitivity, care, and love for an often forgotten group of parishioners. She says that she is energized by the morning's work and by the occasional notes of appreciation from the shut-ins. She has developed a very special ministry.

Unfortunately, such sensitivity cannot be learned. The person who has it and uses it well can be extremely effective. But, at the same time, that person may be open to being hurt. And, often, that hurt can run very deep and come from many sources and directions. For example, by choosing to help another person through a difficult situation, feelings of a similar painful experience from the minister's own life may resurface once again. So, the pastoral associate who has been hurt by one of his or her own children rejecting the values and the love that the family has given to him may find that pain rekindled when counseling a parent in a similar situation. When that is the case, it will hopefully cause the associate to be a better, more loving Christian. This can happen by working hard not to allow one's feelings to take over. It is a real risk.

Giving sound but, unfortunately, unwelcome advice to my brother about his daughter, I was hit with the reminder that, as a priest, I couldn't possibly understand the situation since I had no children of my own. That hurt and stunned me into a sullen silence. It was too painful for me to respond to at that moment. But I sure gave him hell about it later on. And, when necessary or when invited, I am still very comfortable in talking with him about his children, usually as a brother, but sometimes as a priest. As care givers, we need to let go of the small hurts. Being sensitive in the best sense of the word is one thing. Growing more and more thin-skinned indicates a potentially serious problem in our ability to continue to care for people.

The sensitive person who chooses to get involved in any number of tasks runs the risk of being tremendously hurt when someone says or does the wrong thing. That cannot but happen when his or her whole heart or soul is involved in a project or relationship. For example, a minister of care who had spent a great deal of time preparing a Sunday liturgy and anointing of the sick wanted it to touch the congregation in a very special way. She was devastated, however, as she was pinning a fresh carnation on one of those who was going to be anointed and overheard someone complaining about all the money she had spent on the flowers. All of a sudden she was no longer able to see the smiles and the joy that the corsages brought to most of the faces. Will she fall back to paper flowers the next year? I would hope not. Her sensitivity was the driving force in wanting it to be a special ceremony that would bring healing to people. Unless this wonderful caring person is able to put that random and small-minded remark out of her mind, her sensitivity could lead to ruin. She needs to keep her feelings in check. It is a balancing act.

What it comes down to, very often, is that we need to realize that we are public figures. Much of our work is often done in front of others. That fact leaves us wide open to all sorts of comments and reactions. When a loving environment has not yet been created for whatever reason, critical comments will flow frequently and easily because of people's insecurities. These are the kind of comments that become all too common. "The lector's voice is too soft." "The music director plays the songs too slowly." "The Eucharistic Minister's dress is not appropriate." "The pastor doesn't visit the hospital often enough." And on and on. Certainly we need to accept criticism when it is valid. But we also need to determine why it occurs when it is not valid. If for some reason, the people to whom we give our attention are not able to accept our love for them, if they are threatened by the economic or social change around them, if they have been treated poorly or uncaringly by those who came before us, we must work very hard at not being hurt by the comments and criticisms that really just mask their own fears or their own pain.

It is a wonderful sign of successful and loving Christian presence when those same people who were quick to criticize begin to change and become more supportive—they start paying compliments: they smile a little more; they involve themselves in the life of the community more; they begin to listen instead of being quick to complain. What happens is that we become less imposing, less of a threat to them, when they begin to realize that our love for them is genuine.

If we are in touch enough with our own lives and who we are, if we can carefully monitor the depth of our feelings and where they are coming from, we will be more effective. But those are very big "ifs." If we don't let people to whom we are ministering hurt us so deeply that we find ourselves either pulling away from our work in general, or worse, lashing out at them in particular, then we position ourselves to respond better and more sensitively to their needs. It takes hard work, honesty with ourselves, and security in ourselves as Christians to keep from being dragged down to the same level as those who hurt us. Instead, we are able to bring them up to the level of trust, care and love that we show them, at least sometimes.

We must use our sensitivity as a means of making ourselves more effective rather than as a source of hurt. To put up all sorts of walls and barriers to keep from being hurt takes away from the good we might be able to accomplish. As one caring and effective minister put it, "I know that I cannot experience the incredible highs in my life unless I allow for and know that there will be low times as well." Some hurt we must accept. However, when we in positions of care find ourselves hurting instead of loving and supporting each other, it is most damaging, and not just to us, but to our people who see or sense it happening and are left confused or scandalized. This is a very special concern that will be taken up in the next chapter.

One solution to the paradox of remaining both sensitive

DO YOU LOVE ME?

but relatively unscathed is for us to cultivate strong and genuine friendships and support groups. This will be discussed in a future chapter as well. But it needs to be mentioned here in this context. No one needs to suffer hurt in misguided, heroic isolation. Sharing pain with a group of sympathetic peers, or being able to laugh about it on the phone with a close friend can, if not work miraculous cures, at least put it all in a more comfortable perspective. After being deeply hurt by Judas's kiss of betrayal in the garden, Jesus must have felt some love and support from the impetuous Peter who, not knowing what else to do, pulled out his sword and cut off the ear of the high priest's servant. Despite all that was coming down around him, Jesus had to feel good at that moment because however misguided and, unfortuntaely, for however fleeting a moment, his friend did risk going to bat for him. For Jesus there had to be some comfort there. And at that moment he needed all he could get.

As has already been mentioned, in many ministers there is a strong but often misguided streak of independence, of needing to and wanting to go it alone. And if we are not careful, even the most sensitive among us can become used to being the one who comforts, who consoles, who embraces, who is in control, who speaks the right words at the right time. Difficulties often arise when we are the ones hurting or in pain and the ones most in need of others' care.

Sometimes we are simply afraid to let others care for us when we are in pain.

In many ways it all comes down to the subtle hierarchical structures that we have created around ourselves. It is almost as though we are afraid of somehow losing our identity if

83

we allow others to respond to our needs. We must always remember that before we are ministers we are human beings with feelings, with histories, with the same potential to feel pain as anyone else, and perhaps even more. We can and do become sick, our parents may die, loved ones may be diagnosed as having cancer, good friends may move far away, a child of ours may be found using drugs, a spouse may develop emotional problems. To admit to any of these problems, or to let others find out about them, we fear, may somehow diminish us in the eyes of the people we serve. But if we truly love them, it is only fair that we allow them to love us in return and in some situations to minister to us. Love is a relationship. And a relationship is reciprocal. It does irreparable harm to the relationship to reject these overtures just to protect our own fragile self-perceptions. It is by far the better and more human response to accept the gratitude people want to show us when they reach out to help us at those times when we may need to be comforted.

Consider this example:

A woman who had the energy, despite a busy and time-consuming career, to spend more than a year chauffeuring an elderly woman to church and shopping for her a couple of times each week found herself laid up in the hospital with a serious back injury. It was difficult for her because she was used to being active. Her elderly friend found the situation so disturbing that she called the rectory and demanded that the priest visit the woman in the hospital. Not only that, the priest was expected to pick up the elderly woman as soon as he hung up the phone and bring her with him. Imagine the feelings the woman must have had when she looked up

DO YOU LOVE ME?

from her hospital bed and saw the elderly woman who she was so used to taking care of hobble into her hospital room carrying a bunch of beautiful flowers, some home-made cookies and a few well worn back issues of *Reader's Digest* to help her pass the time. Reflecting on it after she was released from the hospital, she said that her initial reaction when she saw the elderly woman was to pull the bed sheet over her face and protect herself from embarrassment. Instead, she fortunately followed her better instincts and allowed herself to feel a tremendous sense of satisfaction, of a job well done, because she obviously meant so much to this woman. And so, she was able to gratefully accept the concern and the love that was being offered to her. It's a safe bet to say that those two women felt better about themselves and about each other after that reversal of roles.

In my first year of priesthood, my grandmother died during Holy Week and had to be buried on Easter Monday morning after being waked on Easter Sunday night. The marathon of Holy Week and my family crisis left me literally speechless. My voice barely lasted to the final commendation at the end of the Mass of the Resurrection. Returning to the rectory very late that night there were two items awaiting me on the floor of my room. The first was not at all unexpected. It was a note from the pastor telling me that he was already gone, since Tuesday was his day off. He reminded me that I was on to celebrate the morning Mass and not to forget, given all that had happened. So much for his sensitivity. Fortunately, next to his note, there was another note indicating that the thermos on the floor was courtesy of the nuns in the convent. It included orders from them that I was to rest my voice, drink the "medication" and get a good night's sleep. They had even gone so far as to have called a priest from the neighboring parish to take care of my morning Mass without feeling the need to clear it with the pastor. Did I even for a moment consider turning down their expression of concern for me? No way! I gratefully drank down the contents of the thermos and slept until noon the next day. It brought the nuns and me closer together. No one ever felt the need to let the pastor in on it.

A bonding occurs when, for whatever reason, we who are in pain take the risk and allow others to show us their love and concern. It is almost as though we shed some of the mystique that we are cloaked in and become surprisingly human. And when that humanity is shared, people are naturally more comfortable in allowing us to return to ministering to them at the appropriate time. Together, they have shared something special. It takes humilty to recognize when we are in pain and hurting. It takes even greater humitity to allow someone to minister to us when we're supposed to be the helper. But it is precisely this humility that touches other people and brings about healing and it allows us to be even more effective. When we reject the outreach of others, we create a separation rather than the bonding that could have occurred.

I remember one pastor who went to great lengths to hide and protect the fact that his father had been recently hospitalized and diagnosed as terminally ill. Despite all that the family was going through, the priest kept every appointment. He did not fall behind on a single task in the parish. He fulfilled every pastoral obligation that he had. When his father finally died, he let it be known to the staff that the wake and the funeral would be private and their presence was neither expected nor desired. Most of the parishioners would not hear about it until the following Sunday. By that time the funeral should be over and everything back to normal. Clearly he was proud at how little disruption his personal concern had caused the parish. He was so proud, in fact, that he was unable to see the added distance that his actions had placed between himself, and other members of the parish staff, and many of the parishioners. There was an almost palpable sense of betrayal that he failed to recognize or feel. They were hurt that they were not allowed to share their concern for him. In his own mind, he had remained always the pastor and that was what was most important to him.

In no way am I advocating that we should or need to wear our hearts on our sleeves and share with an almost pathological delight every personal concern and pain that we have experienced in the past or are currently experiencing. That would become very burdensome. Such efforts easily deteriorate into an immature and unfair attempt to hook people into a relationship through their pity or their feeling sorry for us. Healthy, sustaining relationships cannot be formed in that way. Such attempts can also become very narcissistic ways for us to revel and spend excessive time on our own concerns. Visiting a sick parishioner in the hospital is not the appropriate time for us to show off the scars of our own surgeries or give lengthy descriptions of a current ailment. Rather, it is a time to listen, to comfort, to hold, and to pray with someone who needs to feel more than the doctor's cold stethoscope. What is needed is simply our warm love.

Our preference as ministers should rest clearly with being

human and sensitive over being professional but distant. There is absolutely nothing wrong with crying with people. How can we remain dry-eyed when the retarded and premature baby is allowed five minutes outside the incubator to be held by the parents so that the sacrament of Baptism can be administered? And shouldn't the person who has just buried a loved one be able to use those feelings to better reach out at a wake or a funeral or a burial even when the grieving people are not personally known to the minister? Life's experiences should help us to be better ministers if we are not afraid of the emotions they release.

Scripture tells us that a sensitive Jesus wept at the death of his close friend Lazarus. Judas's betrayal, Peter's denial, the rich young man who chose not to follow him—many situations must have brought Jesus to tears. Scripture also shows us a Jesus with the sensitivity to raise the widow of Naim's son from the dead, unasked, and feed the hungry multitude on the hillside, and heal the man too crippled to reach the miraculous pool in time. If we are as sensitive, the hurts and the pain that we encounter in life, far from destroying us, can strengthen us in our work. There is some risk. But we need not fear. Jesus was never afraid to love. Neither should we be if we desire to be the best, that is, the most effective ministers we can be.

CHAPTER 7

"Do you understand what I just did for you?"

To minister together

SO FAR we have dealt with our relationship with those whom we serve and with ourselves. Our response to others, however, does not take place in isolation. It is crucial to concentrate a bit on those with whom we share the privilege of ministry. It is an area of great concern. In fact, if the larger church is to keep itself from crumbling like an ancient Roman ruin and collapsing from within, those of us working in ministerial roles had better get our act together among ourselves or it may be all over. Good people are trying hard to work together in ministry. But forces from within, our personalities and time pressures, and external forces, like diocesan and Vatican pronouncements, cause even the best-intentioned people to struggle. Certainly, out of such pain there can be growth. But all too often when we cannot creatively and peacefully work together it's the people of God who suffer. And that just should not happen. I hesitate to use the following example. But it is all the more compelling when we realize that problems like these often cannot be solved, even by the best among us.

A particular parish has developed the reputation after years of hard work as being one of the premier parishes of the diocese. In fact, its story of regeneration and renewal has been spread far and wide in many Catholic periodicals and books. The tremendously enlightened pastor had made the commitment early on to give the church to the people and over the course of a dozen years he succeeded marvelously in doing so. The response of the parish community was overwhelming. People returned to church who had been away for decades. Young adults in particular surprised even themselves by making real and genuine commitments to church. The growth of the parish culminated in a successful two-million-dollar-plus renovation and development program that was designed to coincide with the pastor's retirement. Over the years, he had gathered together a vigorous and competent staff of women and men committed to ministry and to involvement in the life of the parish. They had succeeded on many levels and so there were truly reasons to celebrate. A week of rededication ceremonies was scheduled upon the completion of the work in the church. Unfortunately, the pastor fell seriously ill and was hospitalized during all the festivities. Everyone in the parish felt the loss of his presence for the celebrations at which the community intended to also express its affection and gratitude toward him.

Consequently, those became extremely heady and busy days for the staff. And that is precisely how the difficulty arose. A group with tremendous talent, diverse backgrounds, varied skills, and, alas, a presumed openness, found themselves without focus. Unasked, the associate pastor took over the group, issuing memos, granting interviews with the press, making decisions. His intentions were good, but the group itself never had the opportunity to discuss the restructuring of leadership. So, because he was an ordained priest,

DO YOU LOVE ME?

it simply appeared that the leadership automatically passed to him. Neither the female pastoral associate, nor anyone else on the staff questioned or challenged him on his role. But neither did they affirm it as a group.

The dynamics of what happened in that group at that moment in time and how it affected each of them individually is not at all very clear. But what is evident is the fact that many parishioners heard about it, were upset by it for a variety of reasons and, felt angry toward the associate pastor about it. The twelve years of growing trust, of genuine sharing, of expanding openness that the team had woven together so beautifully began to unravel much too easily and much too quickly. It was a frightening process for anyone working to create a united staff, witnessing their faith and working together as equals.

In this situation there is really no one to blame. Questions are easy to ask. Why hadn't the group selected a leader? Why didn't the pastoral associate assert herself? Could she have? What compelled the associate pastor to step right in? And why were so many of the involved parishioners so upset when they heard about it? Did the associate pastor ever really understand his role in the parish and what the people felt about him? Had the staff ever been honest with him? Did they accept, condone, or ignore what was happening? A lot of questions will go unanswered. But they all point to how closely those involved in ministry are watched by the people whom they serve. It was a parish that was justifiably proud that women and men ministered together comfortably, that sexist language had been eliminated from liturgy, that they were not weighed down by an overpowering and debilitating hierar-

Dominic Grassi

chical structure. And so the events of those staff meetings more than just symbolically challenged them all and their vision. The parish and many in it were forced to do some serious soul searching. The good news is that the strength and vitality and vision of so many of them saw the parish through that crisis and their future remains bright and vibrant.

The point of this example is not to pass judgment on the parish, the pastoral team, or any individual. After all, they are doing better than many others. Rather, the point is that even in what can be considered the best of situations, with the most enlightened of people involved, it still takes a great deal of effort to be sensitive to the equality and to the humility necessary for effectively sharing ministry.

And this most certainly is the center of the issue—ministry must be shared. It can neither be hoarded or protected. Those of us in parish service need first of all to admit our insecurities about ourselves and about our roles. Our self-image needs to be strengthened. This is nothing to be ashamed about. It is simply a matter of fact. And it shouldn't really surprise any of us, either.

On the one hand, ordained ministry is viciously under attack from many sources. The media almost revels in the sensational tales of perversion and corruption they report. Bitter people label as clericalism anything done by the clergy that they do not agree with. Many people served by the clergy delight in gossiping about them simply because they are not capable of grasping the charisma of celibacy. To them, priests must be ''fooling around on the side'' with either a woman or another man. How frustrating these attitudes can become for clergy who are trying to do the best they can.

DO YOU LOVE ME?

On the other hand, it must be noted that parish staff who are not ordained fare no better. Limited on the one side by hierarchical structures that they cannot break through and on the other by a frequent lack of acceptance by the people they are trying so hard to serve, they are often frustrated and understandably angry. There is the constant questioning by others and by themselves of their motives. How overwhelming these issues must become for those who are trying to find their place in the church.

It is no wonder that so many people in positions of parish service or ministry—ordained priests and lay associates, employed and volunteer—are so insecure. It would seem to make sense that we see the need to support each other for our own mutual good. Instead, to protect our own fragile self-image, we are constantly on the attack, either verbally abusing each other or, worse, setting all types of road blocks in each other's paths. This is a bleak description. Mercifully, there are exceptions. And they provide us with positive examples that we can imitate and make our own. Sometimes very small efforts are all that are needed.

A few years ago, a pastor with a large and beautiful Gothic rectory chose to move himself out of the pastor's suite of rooms with their vaulted ceilings, leaded-glass windows, and floor-to-ceiling fireplace. He quietly moved himself into smaller quarters. He then converted his former apartment into a space for private reflection and prayer for the entire parish staff. He encouraged not only those who lived in the rectory, but all those involved in the parish to use the space as they saw fit. It not only provided a welcome place for respite for many people, but it very quickly transformed the rectory into a genuine parish house and resource center. In a simple way, that pastor exhibited the sense of equality and humility necessary for faith and service to be genuinely shared.

Ours is a culture that thrives on competition. It is the red-blooded, American response to life. It is drilled into us as children and all too often is the key to our success or failure as adults. However, when ministry is genuinely shared there can be no place for competition. There is nothing that can destroy the building of community among people faster than when those who they call their ministers use them as though they were poker chips to be stacked up on their side of the table and counted. The real needs of people are lost in the frenzy of ministers climbing over each other. It is never a pretty picture.

However, when Christians are capable of sharing a common vision and mission, their own personal success, their numbers and statistics, become unimportant. Is having three counseling appointments in one evening better than spending the time needed to really help one person? What remains most important is that all those involved in parish life work together for their common goals. They must take the time to develop realistic and workable mission statements that can be incorporated into everyone's ministry. It also means not allowing some of the staff to go off on their own with little or no regard for the larger picture. If Father insists on preparing a couple separately for the baptism of their child instead of sending them through the parish preparation program he had better have a good reason for doing so. And he had better feel the obligation to communicate it to the proper people.

DO YOU LOVE ME?

If he doesn't, the legitimacy of the program and of those running it becomes suspect, motive easily become blurred, and ill feelings develop.

If those who are working together—or more likely, separately—in a given setting, feel the need to announce that they are doing more than, or are better liked than, or are dealing with more substantive concerns than others, there is a problem with that group that will have to be worked out if they are to function effectively. Such competition speaks of a high level of insecurity that points to a problem among themselves. Such problems cannot be ignored. They need to be faced honestly. The lector who must announce that he is always scheduled to be the narrator of the Passion on Holy Saturday, the pastoral counselor who slowly but methodically transforms a commonly used office into her own private domain without concern for others who need to use that space, the associate pastor who brags to parishioners that he is asked to witness more weddings than the pastor—all these are symptoms of staff problems that must be dealt with. This is the case whenever our own good has grown more important than that of the people we are expected to be serving. When this happens we need to ask some basic questions once again.

Has the staff with this kind of problems and concerns ever met to pray together? Are there support systems built into its structure? Is there acceptance of each other and respect for the jobs being done and challenges to those who show otherwise?

Parish staffs and all those involved in the parish need to meet regularly to renew their common vision and to work through the human problems that inevitably arise from the pressures of work. Such times need to be set regularly and well in advance. It goes without saying that attendance should be mandatory. And these larger gatherings need to be augmented by more frequent smaller meetings of those who share common ministries or whose activities touch each other and overlap. For example, the ministers of care who visit the homebound should not only meet among themselves, but they should also meet with those responsible for hospital visitations and those who make Communion calls. Prayer, openness, a genuine desire to listen and to learn must be items on the agenda.

Recognition needs to be given to jobs that are well done. We are only human and it can help to blunt our competitive edges. Parish bulletins contain so much that is trivial and unimportant. A good way to bring a staff and a parish together is by regularly showcasing particular groups or activities in the pages of the bulletin, or by thanking individuals or groups at the appropriate time—like the ministers of care on the weekend a liturgy for the anointing of the sick is being celebrated.

A parish named in honor of St. Terese of Avila presents an annual award on the Sunday closest to her feast day to a woman whose presence in the parish exhibits the vision and compassion and leadership that is their patron saint's legacy. It is a way of stating clearly the importance placed not only on one person's ministry, but on that of all who are working hard in that parish. Let's face it, there are more than enough opportunities to reward people and give them the recognition they deserve than just the annual parish sports banquet.

DO YOU LOVE ME?

It is so unfortunate that instead of spending the time and the energy and the resources supporting and celebrating those whose ministries are making such positive impacts on the people, we insist instead on appeasing the irate individual or working around a splinter group that insists on doing things its own way and brings down everyone else in the process. Perhaps it is because by nature ministers are healers and compromisers. Confrontation does not come easily, even when it is obviously and painfully necessary. It is easier to walk away from the problem or to try to cover it up in some way. And so energies get sapped and behavior develops into classical passive/aggressive patterns.

If there are methods of evaluation and feedback that can be built into a staff's structure then those who become overly competitive or grow negative in their outlook will be forced to face those issues. Such a set-up allows them the opportunity to grow and to change their behavior or to make the decision of removing themselves from part or all of their ministry. And if those options are not taken, then there should be a clear process in place for termination. There has to be a better way to deal with the lector who never shows up than assigning a regular standby "just in case." Likewise, there needs to be a better way of dealing with the celebrant whose homilies are never prepared than just avoiding the liturgies that he celebrates.

The question may legitimately be asked, "Why bother with all of these structures? There isn't enough time for ministry as it is." We bother, quite simply, because the people we serve deserve the very best from us. We must concentrate our energies on loving them and not on time-consuming, life-sapping intrasquad squabbles and issues. There is not enough time or energy to devote to both. And while meetings and evaluations are time-consuming and can be difficult, they are far better than destructive alternatives.

The issue of collegiality, of witnessing our faith together, of sharing ministry, must be dealt with on a larger scale. In the American Catholic Church, for numerous reasons, there are too many who have turned ministry into an "either/or" battle—they either reject those who are ordained or they cannot accept lay people—rather than an "and/also" sharing of responsibility—ordained ministry has its place as does lay ministry. This either/or stance will destroy the church.

I know of a Catholic University that over the years has developed an outstanding institute for those interested in pastoral concerns. It has a history of doing an excellent job of training a great variety of people for a tremendous variety of tasks within the framework of church. In some ways it prides itself in being "anti-clerical," and that certainly is not bad at all. Its director, who is a priest, is always pictured in a sportscoat and tie, "one of the guys." Such an image of anti-clericalism is certainly good. It helps break down those hierarchical structures and barriers that have already been mentioned. However, if the feeling moves from anti-clericalism to anti-ordained priesthood, it could be very hurtful not only to priests, but also to the people who ultimately need to be served by a variety of people. The larger church is also hurt. Have no doubt about it.

The problem goes both ways—there exists as much "anti-lay involvement" feeling as "anti-ordination" feeling. Consider this situation. In a diocese divided into parish clusters

DO YOU LOVE ME?

that met regularly and were represented at the Priest's Senate by an elected member, a priest senator who was a pastor announced at a monthly cluster gathering that he would resign as senator and boycott the meetings if a certain female pastoral associate from one of the parishes remained in attendance. Obviously, times had changed. When the configuration of cluster senatorial districts was first created the parishes' ministerial staffs consisted solely of priests. And while a broad spectrum of issues were discussed he felt the meeting would lose something if non-priests were allowed to attend. His insensitive comments were made in the woman's presence. Instead of supporting her right as a pastoral associate to be in attendance, the cluster members unfortunately decided to put it to a vote at the next meeting. Rather than cause embarrassment, she voluntarily removed herself from future meetings.

No wonder there is such painful alienation and such a deep lack of trust among so many of us. Instead of the support needed to help us all function as best we can, our energies get turned inward as we nurse the hurts and try to cover our growing insecurities. There are some attempts on the larger front to deal with this important issue. But they don't go far enough and often are contradicted by other structures. I know of one diocese where lay ministers and deacon candidates are now being trained together. This shows an admirable openness by the directors of those programs. Such combined training of men and women who will ultimately be working together makes sense. But in that same diocese, the major seminary theologate program is limited to male, celibate candidates for the priesthood. Not only is it a tremendous waste of resources, but it also isolates the very ones who need to learn the meaning of collaboration if their priesthood is going to be effective.

It goes without saying, or at least it should, that the greatest resource the church possesses is its personnel, those who are willing to make the many sacrifices necessary to be loving and effective ministers. Yet, in most dioceses most of the time, the energies, and the professional staff deal with money issues, building concerns, resulting in a flood of unnecessary memos and directives. Clearly our priorities are dead wrong.

In many parts of the world, the church is encouraging efforts to expand and become inclusive rather than exclusive and hierarchial. The success of the base communities in Central and South America is a prime example. Yet even though these communities have empowered the poor to take hold of the Gospel and to use it both to grow spiritually and politically, their efforts are being condemned and undermined by those who fear their power. In cases such as these and wherever and however people begin to realize their role in being church to each other, we must show our support and not back down at attempts to subvert such efforts.

Certainly our insecurities make us overly competitive. But perhaps it is also part of our human nature, as well. Even among the disciples of Jesus such temptations and limitations existed. James and John both wanted to sit at Jesus' side when he came into his kingdom. Jesus responded to them immediately with words of warning that following him was tough but were they up to it. He also responded over the longer haul by his example of serving others. After washing their feet, he asked the disciples if they had understood what he

DO YOU LOVE ME?

had done for them. He had given them a final reminder to be willing to serve others with their lives. This is discipleship. This is ministry. This is what we are called to. And he asks us the same question.

Above all else, if we are going to be Christians who serve and love the people of God, it is of paramount importance that we also see ourselves as serving each other. We are no better than anyone else. Our tasks are no more exalted than any others. We must constantly realize that to serve others is a privilege that should humble us. If what we do is for some kind of self agrandizement, if we insist on competing with each other, there is no humility. And, more importantly, there is no love. And without love, as St. Paul tells us, no matter how capable and talented we might be, we are only clanging gongs, too often clashing noisily with each other, doing very little good.

The challenge is to concentrate our efforts on how we can best serve the people of God as Jesus teaches us while at the same time realizing that we cannot do it unless we are willing to accept each other and support each other's efforts. If we can make it happen where we are, we both challenge and stretch the larger church. It cannot and will not be able to ignore the groundswell of good being performed by Christians of all kinds willing to work together.

CHAPTER 8

"Have you not read, 'You shall not tempt the Lord, your god' "

Prayer and reflection

IT HAS taken me sixteen years of priesthood and a whole lot of lip service before I could finally understand and appreciate the valuable and necessary role that prayer must play in our lives. There was no bolt of lightning, no life-changing retreat. All it took was a good and dear friend who moved a half a world away from my world to follow the call to service that had beckoned him for years.

After more than a decade of priesthood in the inner city, after pastoring and coordinating ministry for an entire city area, after consolidating schools and opening retreat centers, after being called on the carpet by the chancery for not translating his work into the cold facts and figures they demanded, Tom had had enough. He decided to scratch the itch that had been with him since well before his ordination. He made the choice to become a Maryknoll Associate and take his vision of church and his love for people to Africa. Not surprisingly, the bishop initially said no to his request. Even less surprisingly, Tom persisted and won. Even a badly broken ankle (requiring the insertion of six pins) shortly before his departure would not and did not deter him.

With close to three months between the completion of his last assignment and his reporting date to Maryknoll—the diocese having left him in limbo—I prevailed upon him to stay at the rectory in which I was living. Certainly, it was not all altruism on my part. As a new pastor, I used his wisdom and his ear on almost daily walks to help me adjust. We grew as close as I thought we could ever become as good friends. Our good-byes were bittersweet because of impending loss and at the same time celebrations of dreams about to be fulfilled.

When he left all of his friends, he began a network of monthly letters that would go out to some 200 or so people, each getting a copy typed and mimeographed and mailed out by a couple to whom he sent the initial copy. These epistles were augmented by personal letters to those of us who wrote back to him. He committed himself to sharing his missionary experience with as many people as possible. His journey initially took him to New York. From there, after months of theological training and language lessons in Swahili, he departed for Africa. After more months of cultural and language training, he finally arrived at a village among the very poor people of Kenya, a remote and dangerous area called "a real mission" by many veteran Maryknollers. Once there, his letters to us changed noticeably. Less chatty and much more reflective, they took on the urgency of wanting to communicate the reality of his experience with us. In one letter he used simple calculations to help him figure out that his 6:30 AM morning prayer lined up exactly at what would be our 10:30 PM Central Daylight Savings Time night prayer.

Realizing that we were actually able to join in prayer at the same time has made 10:30 PM important prayer time for me. Simply stated, I am able to feel closer to him now than when we lived under the same roof, ate our meals together, walked, talked, laughed, and played together. Our common prayer time has brought us together again even though physically we are continents apart. He in his simple, primitive shack and I in a very comfortable rectory are able to come together in prayer. The same stars that I am barely able to see because of the bright lights and pollution of the city and that are fading in his bright, clear early morning sunlight link us to our God who hears us and so link us to each other. The troubles and the concerns that I present to God I now often find to be insignificant as I reflect on the life and death realities being dealt with by my good friend. It is at these times that my thoughts often evolve into genuine prayers of thanksgiving for my many blessings and prayers of concern for Tom and his ministry. My own letters back to him in Africa have grown more reflective, as I share with him the concerns of my prayers.

In prayer, my thoughts often direct themselves to Tom as well as to God. I can use words like solidarity, intimacy, and wholeness to describe this, but they are insufficient. I simply call it prayer shared, a genuine Communion between me and God, me and Tom, and Tom and God. This prayer has clearly affected my ministry in so many ways. It has thankfully allowed me to put it all in better perspective. And it has allowed me to become more trusting of God and more open to God's working in my life. Too bad that it has taken me this long to appreciate what should be central in every life—prayer.

If we are going to love the people we serve, it follows that we must experience the reality of being loved in our lives.

DO YOU LOVE ME?

If we are going to share the love of God with those same people, it also follows that we must experience that same love of God in our hearts. The only way this can happen is through prayer.

But many of us are so busy with our work that we can find precious little time to spare for anything. The temptation is either to pray only during those rare occasions during which we find ourselves with nothing else to do, so that it becomes a kind of filler for chronic workaholics. Or we fool ourselves into thinking that we are praying more than we really are. We tell ourselves, and we really believe, the work we do, the time we spend visiting the sick or listening to someone's problems or writing an article for the parish bulletin or doing so many other things, that these times are prayer if we simply offer them all to God. Certainly there is something to be said for consecrating all that we do to God. But for it to be prayer takes much more because prayer itself is so much more complex.

Scripture presents us with the example of Jesus who went off into the desert or deep into the garden or up to the mountain to pray. Jesus found it necessary and important to leave his healing, his preaching, his miracle working behind and to retreat and pray. It needs to be noted that quite often these times of prayer were not serene islands of peace for Jesus. Very often they were times of struggle with temptation and with doubt about himself, challenging times. But these times can be contrasted with those when Jesus prayed for people to whom he was ministering. Those times were filled with great love and affection. Jesus even referred to his people as sheep searching for a shepherd. And at still other times,

Jesus could be found praying with those with whom he shared his mission. It was at one such time that he gave all of us the beautiful prayer that addresses God as "Abba" or "Daddy." We have unfortunately formalized such a loving and personal expression into the wooden greeting of "Our Father." Our task is to imitate Jesus. We are expected to pray as he did. We need to pray sometimes alone, sometimes with and for those we serve, and at other times with those who share our work. Looked at in this way, it is a lot of praying that is expected of us if we are going to be the loving Christians we are called to be.

It all begins with solitary prayer. But that can be the most troublesome of all. However, it is most necessary for ministers. It is the basis upon which our entire prayer life rests. For unless we are in loving touch with our personal relationship with God, we can neither help others, nor join nor lead them in prayer. Praying alone can often be difficult because when we genuinely center ourselves and so open ourselves up to God and listen rather than feel the need to do all the talking, we place ourselves in a very vulnerable position. We have set up a scenario where not only God can enter our hearts, but also doubts, fears, and insecurities. We may not hear what we want to hear. But ultimately the risk is worth the reward. We will never be more effective with people as at those times when, after prayer and reflection, we are finally able to say with genuine confidence, "Your will be done" and mean it and, further, be able to act upon it.

A very intense and involved priest, suffering from a potentially serious illness found himself in a hospital bed receiving blood transfusions. Like so many people in similar situations, he felt himself more alone than he could ever remember in his life. But instead of letting it become a frightening and alienating experience, he was able to use prayer to help himself deal with it. In his prayer he was able to picture Jesus sitting on the chair next to his bed, reaching out and taking his hand. Praying with that image he was able to feel a tremendous sense of peace come over him. He genuinely felt that he was no longer alone. He believed that he would be able to make it through that dark night, and much more, because Jesus was and would be with him. And now when he is reaching out to those who are even more sick than he was, he is able to bring them to find that same Jesus present with them at their bedside. Because of his personal prayer what a tremendous gift he has received and is able to share with those he visits. He has done himself and continues to do others much good.

Most of us do not often find ourselves caught up in such personal crisis situations. And so we have to consciously work at making the time for personal prayer, especially when things are going well for us. We also must find the format that is comfortable for us. For some it may be traditional times and methods like a morning prayer or just before sleep at the end of the day. Others of us find personal prayer a continuous struggle and need to become more creative about it.

A minister of care uses the drive to various hospitals as the time to pray for those whom she is about to visit. She then uses the trip home to prayerfully reflect on what had happened while she was there. A lector comes to church a half hour early on those days he is scheduled to proclaim God's Word and spends that time alone in a pew praying about the reading he will be sharing with the community. There are countless ways and times and opportunities for private prayer if we see it as a priority. The hows and the whens will vary greatly, but the need for it must remain a constant.

We need to admit and to believe that God will not touch others through us unless we in prayer allow God to begin by touching us. This can be a very tough proposition because in order to become transparent enough for others to find our God in and through us, we must in our prayer be able to honestly see ourselves as we really are. And that is never an easy thing to do. But when we let go and allow our God to love us, more concretely, when we finally can work out our angers and our frustrations and our jealousies and our fears by our genuine praying so that we can be open to God's love, then others will be able to find God's love for themselves through us.

The experience of the Transfiguration of Jesus when he took three of the disciples to the mountain to pray with him is the same miracle that can happen to us. Indeed, others will be able to find our God in and through us. They will come in contact with the specialness that is in us because personal prayer has the power to transfigure us if we open ourselves up to it.

Ministering to others is a particular calling and gift. For those of us in active service of others, personal, private prayer can neither be the ultimate goal we are trying to achieve nor our sole method of praying. This may not be the case for others. Those who have dedicated their lives to contemplative prayer may very well be in a different situation. There is no arguing that they are needed in our world. But the private and personal prayer life of people actively involved with those to whom they are ministering must have a goal that goes beyond the relationship that develops between themselves personally and their God. Such prayer must ultimately lead them to being comfortable praying with and for those to whom they are ministering. Personal prayer becomes both an end and a means.

A newly appointed pastor found himself on hospital calls with the parish secretary because she knew those who were sick personally and he did not. He found himself amazed by her ability to draw together all those who were caring for and visiting the sick to take part in prayer. She gathered them all around the bed, even inviting any of the nurses who might be present, and after she verbalized her prayer, she then invited each person one at a time to share their prayer. If the ill person was able to, she would even have that person share a final prayer with the group. The impressed pastor reflected on all those he had visited over the years in hospitals and how so very often prayer was little more than a final tag-on at the end of the visit rather than the focal point it could and should be, as she had so beautifully demonstrated. Only later did he come to learn the depth of her own personal prayer life.

Praying with and for those to whom we minister is important for a number of reasons. First of all, prayer is able to help both ourselves and the people with whom we are praying to focus on what we are doing together. It is essential that we try to keep the primary goal of all our tasks in clear and sharp focus. And that is the realization of God's saving love working in and through us. People come to us to find

Dominic Grassi

God's love not because we are great orators, sensitive listeners, insightful counselors, or dedicated workers. We must never lose sight of the fact that we are able to reach out to them precisely because they are looking for more than the person that we are. God's love in our response to them deals with more than just their marital problem or just their grief or just their fear. Our task is to affirm them and so to respond to persons whole and entire, not to just one part of their body or psyche or soul that may be hurting. By responding to them with our caring and concerned love we allow God's love to touch and heal them. Our own personal skills can then come into play as a follow up. Praying with them and for them helps us with this process tremendously. It shifts the focus away from us because authentic prayer always humbles. To avoid the temptation of thinking that we, with all our skills and professionalism, are the source of our own success and to keep our focus on those we are serving, we need to pray with and for them so that we know God is working through us. A pastoral counselor who felt that he was experiencing a dry period of very ineffective counseling, almost in desperation began to start each session by praying with his clients. This brought about a focus that both relaxed him and helped the client understand what the pastoral counselor hoped to accomplish. It is now standard procedure with him. Likewise, prayer helps the people to whom we are ministering realize where we are coming from as well as on what our focus with them is based. It helps them not just because we model our beliefs. Rather, by its very transparency, prayer aids us in getting in touch with the presence of God that is in their own hearts and in ours.

110

DO YOU LOVE ME?

A deacon on retreat shared with his colleagues his concern that so many people were asking for his prayers that he was beginning to feel weighted down by their requests. They were asking for prayers for a sick mother or an alcoholic son, for successful surgery or for a favorable job interview, for a safe trip or for a loved one far away. He was being overwhelmed by the many and varied requests. We all recognize that feeling. Being a good and conscientious Christian, he would say that he would of course pray for all their needs. And then he would inevitably feel guilty when he either couldn't remember them all or when he found himself less than enthusiastic in his prayers. So he deliberately began to change his response to their requests.

When people asked for prayers for themselves or for others, he stopped whatever he was doing and invited them to pray with him right then and there. Sometimes the people balked and insisted that he do the praying later for their concerns. But very often, his prayer involved the people by his sharing it with them. And so that prayer helped him help them find and feel God's loving presence.

Praying with people, and for them, serves the function, as well, of creating a trusting relationship between us that goes beyond our personalities and skills. As St. Paul says, it must be Jesus that we preach and not ourselves. Such prayer helps people find the power to care for themselves, to help them heal themselves, to allow them to become less dependent on us and more interdependent with a God whose love they are able to feel. Such moments allow us the opportunity to step back and even out of the picture altogether. It is infinitely better for us instead of being pressured to give

111

answers and solutions to be able to empower people to work with God's loving presence that we have helped them find in their hearts through praying with them.

A pastoral associate earned the enduring gratitude of a family who had just lost its husband and father at home after a long and drawn out illness. All she did was to bring them into the bedroom where he had died, gently pull back the cover that had been placed over his face, and lead them all in a brief prayer. That was all. There was no long sermon about grief and resurrection. She then left them alone together until they were comfortable enough to leave the bedroom. Weeks after the funeral they told her that up to that time she brought them into the bedroom and prayed with them, they were lost in their grief. But after they shared prayer together they all felt a profound peace and a realization that together as a family they would handle their grief and move on. And so they did.

As diverse and as rich as private personal prayer can be, praying with those we are called and blessed to serve can often times prove to be even more awe inspiring to us. There are so many times and opportunities and so many ways that prayer can be our best response. And there are even times when it can properly be our only response. It all follows. If we are comfortable with our personal prayer, we will find ourselves comfortable with prayer that is part of our reaching out to others. For if we feel God's love for us, we can help others feel that same love at those profound moments in their lives.

An ongoing temptation, one that has already been discussed, is our perception of being solo operators, the heroes,

DO YOU LOVE ME?

alone, performing great saving deeds. Such a view is distorted and unhealthy. But when we are able to pray comfortably with those who share our ministry, the sense of working together, of community, of sharing in God's love can become a more powerful reality. Sadly, all too often priests living in rectories are together for years and yet never authentically share prayer. Many of us have experienced parish staff meetings that run three or four hours but have allotted only two or three minutes at the beginning or the end for some perfunctory words that the agenda labels as opening or closing prayers. The insights of faith, the opening of souls, the sharing of hearts that could so greatly enrich our lives are too often overlooked or avoided.

Those who work closely together in a parish need to share prayer for a number of compelling reasons. First of all, sharing prayer enables us to break down walls of distrust or competition that may have arisen. It can help us experience each other at deeper, more beautiful levels and so grow to appreciate each other more. Prayer, if authentic and not just words spoken together, can break down those barriers that may have started to develop in a given group or team or staff. Prayer can help us slow down, something that is always needed, and refocus on what should be real and genuine priorities. And prayer can offer the opportunity for healing and forgiveness to take place when necessary. Prayer with such power must be a priority. It must take all the time that it needs. And it cannot come off of a Xeroxed sheet of paper that is passed around. When such prayer becomes a natural part of our lives together, it can even serve to keep problems from arising.

Dominic Grassi

When those who are sharing ministry choose to pray together, that choice can provide tremendous witness not only to those who are part of the group, but also to a much greater number of people. The impact can be profound. The music director of a very large suburban parish always defined his role in the church community as ministry in the fullest sense of the word. He did not only select songs, rehearse a choir, and make music happen. Being a minister also meant for him to make the choice of inviting and encouraging a paraplegic who had once been a professional singer before he was paralyzed, to sing in the choir. And while the young man's voice was strained and forced because of his disability, to hear him sing from his wheelchair a psalm refrain on trusting the Lord has touched the hearts of many people, perhaps more than a Pavarotti could. As importantly, the opportunity to still be able to communicate with his voice has given his life a meaning that he thought had been taken away from him. That same music director also takes the time necessary at rehearsals with the choir to go over the words of each hymn they will sing. The choir members are invited to share their insights into the meaning of each piece. Those insights then become the focus for prayer even before a single note has been played or sung. Other choirs may sing better. Few can lead the congregation to prayer more effectively.

When we share prayer together, it allows us to focus again on the humbling realization that it is God's love working through our efforts. A commitment to such communal prayer will force us to reflect on our experience in private prayer. And such prayer together can also help us to grow more comfortable in our prayer with the people we are serving. This

114

communal praying can take place at meetings or at special times set aside for prayer only. Days of reflection, evenings of prayer, morning praise—there are many ways to share prayer with quality time reserved for it, if it is a real priority.

For a number of years a high school faculty began their school year with a day of recollection. Despite selecting top quality people to present the day, it was seldom more than an exercise required of all teachers. It was only in the year when the person scheduled to run the day canceled and the administrator asked the faculty to share prayer and input with each other that the day really served its purpose of uniting the faculty in faith. Since that year the faculty has chosen to share together without the help of ourside speakers. It is now a day valued highly by that group.

At this point it would be good to mention and to emphasize the need to find opportunities to pray and to meet with people other than those we are serving. Prayer and support groups are an absolute necessity to help us keep our lives in perspective. Such groups can be set up in a variety of ways. For some, friendship groups might be the way to do it. I know of a group of friends—two married couples and three priests—who have been meeting together for nearly ten years, sometimes monthly, sometimes bi-monthly. They do not work together in the same setting anymore, but they bring many concerns for prayer. They have supported each other in times of sickness, grief, personal failure, spiritual confusion, as well as during times of happiness and peace. The monthly meetings have become points of light at times when prayer may have grown dim in their lives. This group is typical of many. Another, very different group also meets regularly.

Dominic Grassi

A group of pastors, all newly appointed and around the same age, meet on the last Sunday evening of each month with no set agenda or topic. Very often prayer and personal spiritual concern becomes their focus. These are only two examples. What is important is to find people with whom we are comfortable and eager to share prayer and not to see it as another task that must be fit into a busy schedule. Rather, it can be a refreshing oasis, eagerly anticipated, that will be able to sustain us between gatherings.

Prayer has been considered generically in this chapter. Little emphasis has been given to the form that prayer might take. But we as Christians have one prayer that above all others reflects the reality of God's love real and present in our lives and in our world. It reflects our attempt to share that love with others. And that prayer is the Eucharist. In both Word and Sacrament we as Christians are nourished. The very communal nature of the Mass allows us to focus on the saving action and presence of God in our world as it works in and through us and others. So, for all of us, the Eucharist should play the central role in our prayer life.

Unfortunately, for some, but not surprisingly, the Mass as we celebrate it can still emphasize the hierarchical structures that separate us rather than bring us all together. By its very essence the Eucharist should heal and not divide. Bread must be broken and the cup must be shared among equals who together celebrate the Eucharist making God's presence and love a reality in the world. Sensitivity must be used to make sure that we are being inclusive or there is no Eucharist. Only a hollow and hurtful ritual remains.

There is a sad and painful irony in that, even as we admit

to the central importance of the Eucharist in the lives of those who are so intimately involved in people's lives, and indeed in the life of the entire church, that very church in its hierarchical structure is blindly and stoically choosing to limit itself by allowing its celebrants to be only ordained, male celibates. Fewer priests will mean fewer opportunities to celebrate the Eucharist, at least as we do so today. The growing realization that we share a common calling, female and male, married, celibate and single, together with our acting and working together will ultimately be part of the forces the Spirit will use to break down the artificial and limiting structures.

So it is in this time of transition in the church that there is the special need to be people of prayer. Our faith must allow for us to feel God's loving presence, a presence that will help us be healers, and when necessary, prophets at the same time—the topic of the next chapter. The temptations that Jesus faced, the quick fix, problems easily resolved, were overcome by prayer. We need to let Jesus' example be ours. We cannot give in to the temptation to quit. We must respond as Jesus did, with prayer.

CHAPTER 9

"Do you not know that my father's house is a house of prayer?"

To serve is to be prophet

AT FIRST it was fairly easy for her to ignore what she was hearing. As Director of Religious Education in a large, suburban parish, she needed all the help in organizing and staffing the religious education program that she could get. So, while she was uncomfortable, in her mind this justified her ignoring the racial overtones of some of her teachers' comments. The parish itself was situated in an all-white suburb. But that suburb bordered nervously on a section of the larger city that was growing rapidly more African American in its population. Many of the teachers in her program were parents, active parishioners. They were what many would describe as good, honest, hard-working people. But many of them had moved once or twice before from neighborhoods that had recently changed. They thought that by moving into a suburb they were "safe." Now they were nervous and, sadly, their prejudices began to surface more openly. First there were the jokes. And they led to negative comments and finally to open discussions about "those people" and "our problem." The D.R.E. did not want any of this to filter into the classrooms. And for a while it didn't. But all hell finally broke loose when one of the new textbooks referred to Dr. Martin Luther King Jr. as a saint. This became

118

their issue and focal point. She was told by some of the teachers to get rid of the textbook or they would quit. She looked to the pastor for support. He just looked the other way. Alone, she prayerfully decided to confront the issue head on. Clearly the issue was more than what a particular textbook was saying. Calmly she let it be known that the teachers' next in-service session would be given by an African American priest. Attendance would, of course, be mandatory. If they wished to teach, they would have to be present.

Sadly, but not unexpectedly, she lost more than half of her teachers and a large number of students. Certainly she wasn't happy with what had happened. She had been a friend of many of the teachers who had left. And she had genuinely cared about the children. She still had strong feelings for them, but in her heart she knew that she had no other choice. She had acted as she had precisely because of her love for them. She had talked with them individually. And she had met with them as a group. But then she had to follow her conscience. She knew that it would be a situation where there would be precious little healing. She had been called to respond as a prophet to people she loved and to the larger community who watched what was happening. It wasn't easy.

Being prophetic is never easy. In fact, if anyone finds it exciting or even enjoyable to challenge people or to tumble their idols, the danger of demagoguery becomes all too real. While most of the time we are healers, there will inevitably be times when the only way to love people, to share the Gospel of Jesus with them is to take upon one's shoulders the mantle of prophet, to be the one who sees things more clearly, often not by choice, and courageously challenges others with that vision. This can only be done after there has been much prayer and reflection. Very often the time and the place will be dictated by outside forces. But the prophetic response can only come from the heart after such prayer and reflection.

When Jesus entered the temple area and suddenly started to overturn the money changers' tables, scattering coins for eager children to pick up and run home with, when vendors saw their turtle doves flying away released by a very angry Jesus, when those who had greedily herded the sheep and lambs into pens to be sold for ritual slaughter bleated louder than their animals because of Jesus striking them with a quickly made whip, when all this was happening most of those observing it and caught up in it knew who Jesus was. They had seen him and heard him before. He was the familiar healer of the sick. He was the one who raised others from the dead. He was the producer of loaves and fishes to fill the multitude. He was the one who changed water into sweet wine. He had sat on the hillside embracing little children with gentleness and sharing with those who had gathered the simple, enduring wisdom of the Beatitudes. In short, this prophet Jesus was someone who had a history with most of them. And it was precisely because he had cared so deeply for them that Jesus' prophetic action in the temple courtyard had such tremendous impact. There is no doubting that it brought out a lot of anger, especially among those whose self-interest was so openly challenged, enough anger, in fact, to fan the flames that would ultimately lead to the shouts of "crucify, crucify him" from the mob. But we also have to believe that the day after Jesus' actions, the temple area was a little cleaner, a little quieter, and a little more respectful, with slightly lower voices and prices.

Clearly, being prophetic cannot effectively take place, if the one who is being the prophet has not already firmly established the credibility that comes from a history of caring for the people. One cannot be prophet without first being minister to those people. Also, one cannot usually stay prophetic for a very long time. The prophet must return as soon as possible to being the minister or the message grows strident and self-righteous. To me, what makes a Daniel Berrigan such an effective prophet concerned with human life, its value, and its dignity when he spends the morning protesting at a nuclear missile site and then the afternoon protesting at an abortion clinic is not only the brave consistancy of his vision, but also the knowledge that he will return that evening, if he isn't arrested, to caring for men and women suffering with AIDS. He is the perfect example of the prophet who is rooted in his ministry and whose prophetic voice is given credibility because of that commitment.

To be a prophet is never easy. The neatly put together image of ourselves and our role as the great healer who is loved by all will most certainly be shattered. Our very concept of church may be challenged by the call to be prophet. Consider, for example, the pastor who has a genuine sense of openness and a willingness to empower the people of the parish. He set up a structure for the parish council that allowed it the final say in all decisions. He would not veto anything they decided. When the council unfortunately voted to replace the monthly envelope that parishioners received dedicated to helping an inner-city parish as part of a diocesan-wide, mandated sharing program and to replace it with an envelope that would hold donations from people for the building of a new gymnasium for their own parish, he chose to remain true to his word even though their choice was self-serving and clearly wrong. At that moment the people needed a prophet, one who would say "no" to their short-sighted, uncaring interests, one who would challenge them to see clearly that their strong desire for a gym should not preclude their concern for the less fortunate and blind them to the larger picture of what church really is. If the pastor had chosen to be prophetic for even a short period of time, perhaps he could have led the council to see that both a gym for themselves and continued generosity toward others would have been a better, and Christian choice.

Very often we react negatively to the notion that we might somehow have to become a prophet because we identify the prophet as a headline grabbing firebrand or a John the Baptist dressed in the skins of wild animals, eating berries and grasshoppers, wild-eyed and foul smelling. In fact, the most effective of prophets are those who look like and live with those to whom they are called to be prophetic. Given the following descriptions of potential "prophets," who would receive the best response from the people to the request for a generous donation to support Catholic Education and to keep the parish school open? Would it be the professional fund raiser in a three piece suit with a bunch of statistics and figures presented at a meeting? Would it be the pastor with his annual pitch for more money from the pulpit? Would it be a visiting priest chastising the people during a Lenten mission because they have too many creature comforts? Or would

DO YOU LOVE ME?

it be a member of the parish finance committee who had three children graduate from the school and who can speak from the heart to her peers about her own decision to support the school for other people's children and for future generations?

I'd certainly vote for that parent. People seem to be naturally receptive to, or in some cases, most challenged by a voice that comes from one like them. It is much harder for an outsider to be a prophet.

Often times, being the prophet is lonely and isolating. Being a minister is different. When we are sharing our love with people usually there is some kind of positive response to our hard work. People are grateful. But the prophet who must confront people and challenge them, showing them their limitations, can often be isolated as people turn their backs in confusion or in anger.

The youth minister at an affluent suburban parish was clearly successful in her work. She was able to set up a number of well attended programs and activities, both social and spiritual, for the teens of the parish—everything from weekend ski trips to overnight, lock-in retreats. Most of the people of the parish knew her and agreed that she was very good. And so the parish responded positively to her. There were many thoughtful thank-you notes, dinner invitations and generous gifts. But things changed when she decided to introduce a program on drug education for the teens. She found herself meeting subtle, but very real resistance. Many of the parents felt that there wasn't a drug problem in their community. Patiently and thoughtfully she prepared a presentation to show them sadly how wrong they were. Only two parents showed up for it. Quite suddenly, teens stopped receiving permission to attend scheduled outings. Fewer were allowed to attend the retreats. The letters, invitations, and presents stopped coming. After a while, it wasn't very hard for a member of the parish finance committee who was also a disgruntled parent to question her salary. Only a united parish staff who clearly stood beside her and encouraged her, kept her from giving up. She had to start all over again and perhaps will be able to bring up that topic again in the future. Being a prophet has not been easy for her.

In that kind of situation, it is very easy for outsiders to question motives, tactics and issues. The prophet deals with issues that are on the sharp edge and that have the potential for cutting deeply. Often times, being right, the prophet might unintentionally but unavoidably cause some pain and hurt. But if the prophet is wrong, the results could easily be catastrophic. James Jones and Jonestown come easily to mind. That is why the prophet needs to be a person of deep, personal prayer. Prayer will keep the prophet on track by keeping issues in proper focus. To act out of anger, self-righteousness, or vindictiveness is not prophetic. Rather, it is small, limiting, and often sinful. It follows, then, that prophets must always be in clear touch with their motives. Because the prophet is always first of all a healer, the primary motive for whatever is said or done must be the same as Jesus'—a deep and real love for the people who need to hear the message, even if it might be painful to them. We must beware of the so-called prophet whose message is directed to "you people" with "your problems." It is a genuine prophet who speaks softly and with concern of "us" and "our concerns." this does not mean that the prophet is unsure of the message.

DO YOU LOVE ME?

Rather, the prophet's conviction comes from and is nourished by the self-searching that is part of all prayer and from the subsequent certainty that the message must be shared.

The prophet must strive to empathize or "feel with" those who might be stung by the message that is being proclaimed. In the 1960s film *Jesus of Nazareth,* directed, interestingly, by an Italian Communist, Pasolini, the character of Jesus initially is very remote and harsh, a typical 60s radical, until the scene in which he is standing on the hillside, looking down, and prophetically condemning Jerusalem, warning of its destruction. The camera is set behind Jesus' back looking over his shoulder down at the city. We can hear his voice. It is harsh but steady and sure. It is only when the camera slowly pans around to Jesus' face and we are allowed to see the tears streaming down his face showing his deep love for Jerusalem even as he shouts out his prophetic message, it is only at that moment that we are able to realize how very painful and how very lonely it must be to be a prophet.

Most of the time we can and do minister effectively together. But the prophet must remain an isolated figure even in the midst of the people. Two or more people attempting to be prophets and simultaneously preaching the same message tend to be perceived as a clique of malcontents or rabble rousers. And yet left alone by himself or herself, the prophet whose vision initially may have been very clear can easily veer off target, especially when stung by a negative response to an unpopular message. So the prophet needs to have someone who can be of help, a spiritual director, or a mentor, or a confessor in whom to confide. The prophet needs someone who is outside the situation. This person can then be objective as well as stabilizing and can also, most importantly, challenge the prophet to continue to proclaim God's word and nothing less. The D.R.E. mentioned earlier in this chapter was seriously tempted to run a series of scathing articles on racism in the parish bulletin. Fortunately, another D.R.E. from a neighboring parish who was working with her closely helped her to realize that such action would only put her in an even more adversarial role with many of the parishioners and would prove to be nothing more than counter productive in the long run. Positive articles about the dignity of all people and the need for goodness and trust in God would prove to be more effective as time went on.

Being a prophet also means remaining concerned about the many other needs of people, even as they are being challenged by the prophetic message. But the prophet may not be the one to best help people with those needs. So the prophet must gather others who have been ministering to the same people and encourage them to continue to do their work. If prophets don't do this they run the risk of becoming single focused fanatics. Others often are called to initiate the healing process that must occur once the prophet's message has been heard and, it is to be hoped, accepted.

In a large, blue-collar urban parish, for instance, an energetic and idealistic young associate pastor saw a growing need to take care of the increasing number of unemployed and laid-off workers in the community. His focus began initially as ministry, providing temporary work when available or food and clothing when necessary. Inevitably he found himself having to go toe to toe with the employers in the area. Under his leadership strikes were called and management was challenged. The media was brought in and then the politicians naturally followed. Ultimately, concessions were made and people retrained and reemployed. The associate pastor then prudently stepped back and let the community organizers and union representatives be the liaisons and work out the details with the companies. To have kept himself in the picture would have kept the relationship between workers and management adversarial. He wanted the necessary healing to occur. And that would now be best left with others rather than with him. He had been the prophet and would always be identified as such with those people. He chose to continue to work quietly behind the scenes when necessary. He was even able to admit that there were times when he missed the excitement of it all. But wisely he turned his attention to concerns in the parish that allowed him to be the person they needed. When it came time to step back from being the prophet and to become a minister once again, he had made the right decision for many reasons.

Make no mistake about it, there will be those situations, like it or not, when we will be called upon to make the decision to be prophets or to leave it to others. The causes and concerns may not be great headline grabbers. But there are so many ways in which people become wedded to the status quo in their lives. And when that status quo keeps them from living out the Gospel message it needs to be challenged. But remember, it can only be done with love and it can only be done after much prayer. At the same time, we need to be ready to accept the fact, as painful as it may seem, that people will not always respond to us as we would like. But if we choose to be involved in the church, we must also choose at times to be the prophet. The Gospel of Jesus Christ is what we preach. So often it is wonderfully healing, compelling in its power to change lives. But occasionally it is that two-edged sword that can cut so very deeply. But it is what it is. We cannot preach or live only a part of it. It's all or nothing.

In the church in which I am currently privileged to serve, the old-fashioned, high pulpit still rises on the "Gospel side" about a quarter of the way down the aisle soaring majestically over the pews. Beautiful as it is, it is largely ignored now except by a photographer eagerly searching for new angles as he videotapes a wedding. Always looking for a gimmick as a preacher, I thought it would be interesting on the weekend that the readings included the commandments and Jesus with the money changers outside the temple to climb the twelve steps of the high pulpit instead of presenting my homily in front of the altar in my usual folksy style. I would then mention to the congregation how the readings were conducive to the hellfire and brimstone sermons that they had heard in their youth. I would then come back down, take the microphone and walk to my usual spot, telling them that such preaching was not my style and that it would be better to concentrate on God's love of us all. At the first two Masses it all went very well. The ploy received a few laughs, caught people's attention, and made its point. But at the last and most crowded of the Masses I climbed the stairs and when I reached the top, before I could speak a word the congregation broke into spontaneous applause. Having no idea at all what it meant, I stuck to my script. When I came back down and took the microphone to the front of the altar they applauded again. I'd like to think for purposes of this chapter that perhaps they had somehow recognized those few times I had been prophet and those ongoing times I had ministered to them, the pulpit reflecting the prophet and the position up front reflecting the priest. Actually, I still don't know what it really meant. But I am taking it that way until told otherwise. And I will try to continue to function as full-time minister and occasional prophet in my Father's house.

CHAPTER 10

"Whose face is on the coin?"

Social involvement

EVERY once in a while, our journey through life allows us to cross paths with someone we know for certain is so special, so much larger than life, that they become for us genuine heroes. For me, Monsignor Jack Egan is one of those unique people. Before it was fashionable to be a champion of civil rights for minorities and of lay involvement and ownership of ministry in the church, before Vatican II's pronouncements, Jack was part of a remarkable generation of priests who, at first because of the inattentiveness of Samuel Cardinal Stritch and later because of the active support of Albert Cardinal Meyer, brought about a genuine Renaissance in the Catholic Church in Chicago. However, the arrival of the formidable John Cardinal Cody on the scene spelled a return to the Dark Ages—in more ways than one. Inevitably, Jack Egan found himself in exile—if you could call working with Father Ted Hesburgh at the University of Notre Dame living in exile. Not unexpectedly, Joseph Cardinal Bernardin, the great reconciler—and no minor politician—quietly but to some acclaim, brought Jack back to Chicago.

Being the Irish fatalist and romantic that he is and having survived a recent battle with open-heart surgery, Jack thought

DO YOU LOVE ME?

it wise upon his return to gather around himself fifteen or so of the younger clergy of the diocese to share his vision, his insight and, more practically, his contacts because, as he would put it, "I'm not getting any younger, you know." So a very diverse group of men gathered in the auditorium of Holy Name Cathedral on a rainy Sunday evening. Jack made himself available to the group and monthly Sunday evening sessions were set up. Meetings "off the record" with people so diverse as Mayor Harold Washington's Director of the Office of Planning, to a co-ordinator of a highly successful city food pantry and self-help program were scheduled. Unfortunately the group dwindled to just a few priests after a couple of months. Sunday evenings appeared to be too valuable to give up or the people themselves were too exhausted or it just was not a genuine priority for most of them. Inevitably the group disbanded and marvelous opportunities were lost by a group that could have made a tremendous difference armed with the knowledge and contacts that Jack had offered to them.

For whatever reasons, I personally fell under the trance of this exceptional priest. At his invitation I found myself at times stepping into his place—giving the convocation at an anti-nuclear arms rally in Chicago's Grant Park in front of 25,000 people, for one—and regretfully, more often than not, not having enough time to fit other opportunities he offered into my schedule.

An unexpected visit at 11:00 PM by Jack to the rectory with a potential new parishioner for me to sign up, got us to talking about the parish and this book. Jack and his friend had been out to dinner in the neighborhood and, true to his

131

character, Jack felt there was no better time than that present moment to introduce us. I was writing at the time and Jack became very interested. After discussing what I hoped to accomplish and what I wanted to say with this book, Jack stared me in the face, became very serious, almost sad, and said softly, "Don't forget social justice. Don't forget that church goes beyond the parish. We're turning in on ourselves too much."

Immediately, I knew that he was right. And I also knew that I had not planned for such a chapter as this in my outline. I too, it would seem, had fallen easily into the trap of thinking that the church is the parish (or institution) in which I work and nothing beyond that. I had also succumbed to the argument that with the explosion of ministries in the church there is so much for us all to be doing and not enough time in which to get it all done.

That means we have to leave the other concerns to outside groups or agencies. Neither of these positions is valid. And so I thank Monsignor Jack Egan for giving me the impetus to add this chapter. It wasn't so much his words that convinced me. It is his life as a dedicated proclaimer of the Gospel that assured me he is right.

When those who did not want to hear Jesus' message because they knew that it would make them uncomfortable tried to trip him up about taxation, his response was simple and straightforward, "You tell me" Jesus asks patiently, "whose face is on the coin" that they held before him. Jesus uses the opportunity to make a major statement about his message. Certainly there are immediate, spiritual concerns—those things to be rendered freely to God. And there are temporal and worldly concerns—those that need to be rendered right-fully into Caesar. It is important to understand that Jesus does not say that we must ignore those concerns of the world or even that we should let someone else take care of them. Rather, simply, yet powerfully, he balances what we must render to God along side of our responsibility to the world, our brothers and sisters, to whomever needs our help.

What does this mean concretely to those ministers who are attempting to love the people of God as Jesus did? First of all, it means realizing that our work does not and cannot take place solely in the vacuum that we call our parish or institution. Jesus' message, the Gospel, does not allow for that. Rather, all of our various tasks must take into account the world in which we live with its injustices, its pain, its sorrows. That means, concretely, that the member of the liturgy planning committee of a parish who argues strongly against having prayers of the faithful that reflect on social problems of headlines because that would be "too political for church" needs to be reminded that the church at times needs to be political. And it means that the member of the parish School Board who is concerned only with test scores and advancement needs to better understand not only the mission of Catholic Education, but also the imperative of the Gospel to look beyond our own needs and concerns. While our current pope speaks of priests and those in ministry not becoming identified with any particular political movement, certainly his own actions indicate that we in the church are compelled at times to raise some clearly political questions and provide answers that some would label in anger and self-righteousness as political.

Dominic Grassi

In a staff discussion on this very topic, a priest defended the position that the church should not get involved in justice issues because of their often political nature by relating his story of being in the seminary during the turbulent years of the late 60s and early 70s. He indicated that in his mind those among his classmates who went off campus and skipped classes or meetings occasionally to march for civil rights or to protest the war in Vietnam were missing what the church was called to do and to be and, therefore, were counterproductive. He told the group that his choice was to spend time in chapel praying for justice and for peace. That, he felt, was the church's role and contribution to the world. It is difficult to argue against prayer so there was a noticeable silence for a while among all those who had listened to him. Finally, another contemporary priest addressed the group in a quiet, nonjudgmental voice. He spoke of having taken part in some marches and rallies, having attended a few lectures and sit-ins and of having done some leafleting. But he also spoke of making the time for prayer and reflection on all that he had chosen to do. It was not one or the other. Rather the action demanded prayer from him and that prayer was what ultimately led him to action. In all cases the choice is not between spiritual or temporal concerns. Rather, we must respond to both, make the time for both, have the vision to see both no matter how some choose to label it or want to restrict us. The Gospel cannot be restricted.

There is a human temptation to compartmentalize and try to bring order to our busy lives. And so it is natural that Social Justice Committees, Pro Life Committees, the St. Vincent de Paul Society, Peace and Justice Groups, and similar

134

organizations become those that are most often called upon to be either the conscience of a parish or its action wing on justice issues. And, at first glance, this would appear to be the perfect solution. Why not let those who really want to do such work do it and leave the rest of us alone with our other concerns? Such a response, however tempting, is really not much better than leaving the entire parish or institution in a vacuum and so really it is not acceptable. The better response is to find creative ways of involving the entire community. Certainly a social action committee can help to put together a Lenten food drive to help the hungry (either those from the parish itself or elsewhere). Much more can happen. For example, the liturgy planning team could develop a special liturgy to either kick off the drive or to conclude it. A recent Lenten food drive ended with a procession lead by children after Good Friday to a local food pantry. Eucharistic ministers could be invited to organize a bread-baking for the drive. Teachers could discuss the problems of world hunger in the school or C.C.D. program. Children could make posters for the church and school or to place in the windows of local businesses asking for donations of canned goods. Ministers of care could invite those they visit to pray for the hungry and for the success of the drive. Special articles could be prepared for the bulletin. The pastoral associate or deacon could plan special Lenten Friday soup nights combining some simple fasting with adult education. One high school sponsored what was called a Lenten "filmfast" where a plain bread and light soup meal was shared, canned food donated, a film shown, a discussion held, and it was ended with prayer.

Dominic Grassi

When many or all of a group's resources come together on a social justice issue or concern it can serve to both unite and educate people. All of the work coming together can be considered being church on the most profound level. For it can be an opportunity to change peoples hearts and make them more loving.

There is a caution, however, that must be issued. Be our issue world peace or women's rights, be ours a concern for the unborn or for the rights of the elderly, be it those whose needs call out to us as racial minorities or those locked up in prisons—whatever our issues, we must never allow ourselves to become so single minded that we make that particular cause the sole focus of our work. It is the same caution here as was made about being a prophet. Such a focus can often lead to demagoguery and to blindness toward other problems or concerns. Because I am committed to dealing with the plight of the homeless in my community, it does not mean that I am in any way in opposition to those whose concerns focus on the rights of the unborn.

The "seamless garment" ethic proposed by Joseph Cardinal Bernardin should apply across the board to all social justice issues because all of them ultimately deal with life and the quality of living on some important level. There is a sublime and important interconnectedness to be found among all the justice and life issues. They cannot be separated one from the others. And when they are it must be challenged. When the president of a parish's human life commission found it necessary to berate the associate pastor for daring to include nuclear arms, gun control, capital punishment and other issues rather than dealing solely with abor-

DO YOU LOVE ME?

tion in his sermon on Right to Life Sunday, it took a courageous and focused pastoral associate who heard the comments
to sit her down and explain how her very actions were prov-
ing to be contrary to all that her group stood for, not so much
arguing the pros and cons of the issues themselves, but rather,
defending respect for all life.

Clearly it is easy to see why those of us involved in people's
lives in the church unfortunately will often avoid dealing with
such justice issues. It is an area fraught with potential disaster.
Too often we can easily alienate and anger the very people
we are attempting to help and so risk rejection by them. But
such risks must be taken if we are to be true to the Gospel.

On the other hand, it is also very easy to leave behind what
some might consider the mundane, ordinary work of parish
life for the bright lights and fast lanes of involvement in the
social justice concerns that might currently be in vogue. This,
too, is a pitfall that must be avoided at all costs. We need
only to reflect on what was discussed earlier about genuinely being a prophet to understand this concern. A clear sign
that we are moving in the wrong direction is when we begin
to find it necessary to hog the spotlight and do not want
anyone to share in the work we are doing. When our other
work and responsibilities get set aside as uninteresting and,
later, as unimportant, that is a very bad sign as well. When
commitments in other areas are no longer kept, when attendance at scheduled meetings become erratic and appointments
are missed, all because we are concentrating on a single, special issue, we are no longer being effective. And the people
who need us know that they are being shortchanged. The
results of such action, or inaction could be devastating not

only to those who are no longer being served and to those among us who will have to pick up the slack, but also to the very person whose focus has become so single minded. The people who need our love are forgotten. No matter what the cause, no matter what the issue, nothing can ever be more important than our love for the people of God.

If we come across an issue that is so important, that must be dealt with, we need to marshall all the troops and have as many people stand with us and work with us as possible. It becomes our responsibility to enable the people whom we are serving to make the issue theirs as well and to empower them with the confidence, skill, and desire to deal with it along with us. We cannot and must not ever see ourselves as saviors. We are not.

Whenever we deal with issues of justice and the rights of people, we must make sure that both our concern and the concern we hope to generate in people is real, deep, and based on the Gospel. We must avoid fads and using these issues to busy ourselves when other real problems are present. The concern must first of all be a real one. Sometimes causes are "in" because of media hype. That is not reason enough. For example, what brings us to oppose apartheid in South Africa? Have we ourselves experienced oppression? Have we at least shared in another's experience of it? Is all we know about it what we are reading in the papers? Have there been other, more personal ways to glean the knowledge necessary to commit ourselves to this cause? Is our concern evident only at meetings or rallies? Or are we haunted by the injustice and brought to righteous anger and tears of rage regularly as we reflect on the rights that we have and others do not? The concern must be deep.

Is our soul not at rest because of this issue or will we move on to another cause next week? Do we take the time to learn how and what to boycott and divest or do we find that too time-consuming and confusing to deal with? And, finally, is our concern based on the Gospel of Jesus that calls each of us to love one another as sisters and brothers and to realize that whatever harm is done to the very least among us harms, ultimately, all of us because we are all made in God's image? And do we show that concern thousands of miles from South Africa by how we deal with people with whom we come in contact day in and day out?

A member of an affluent parish's finance committee and a respected parishioner who hardly ever made waves traveled to South Africa on business. The trip became one of those once-in-a-lifetime, life-changing experiences. Upon his return he used the forum of the parish finance committee with the approval of the parish staff to address the issue of Apartheid head on. It is important to note that he personally changed jobs before he began to educate the parish through articles in the bulletin as to which corporations still do business in South Africa. He urged parishioners to follow his example and divest themselves of stock in those companies and to actively contribute to helping the poor, if not in South Africa directly, at least somewhere locally. It was because of his witness that the School Board of the parish voted to have the pop machine in the school cafeteria replaced because it was owned by a company that continued to do business in

South Africa. It was replaced with a machine from a company that does not. There were some in the parish who did not respond to him at all. In any case, what was important was that he did what he had to do and by educating people with such conviction, he was able to change some of them as well. In a real sense, he put his money (and lifestyle) where his mouth was. He gave of his own personal substance and not just from the excess in his life. And so, he was able to make a difference. It should be noted that he also was able to help develop a balanced budget for the parish, keeping a broader focus intact.

His story is really an example of how we should respond when it comes to social justice. As much as it must not be allowed to consume us, it also cannot be just a sideline or a hobby to fill up empty time. It is necessary that we model our commitment to social justice by giving from the very substance of our lives—our time, our energies, and our resources. And we must invite the community in which we serve to do the same.

Finally, we must be sure that the message we preach, especially in this important area of social justice, is the message of Jesus Christ. Like the prophet, it must be Jesus we preach and not ourselves, as St. Paul reminds us. And this means taking risks like Jesus did, being firm like Jesus was and remaining gentle as did Jesus.

In an earlier chapter I described a music director whose compassionate sense of church led his choir to become a genuine instrument of prayer for the worshiping community. This same person has touched the entire parish on a different level as well, in an area that would certainly fall under the heading

DO YOU LOVE ME?

of social justice. The parish where he works is suburban. Many of the people in it fled once, twice, and often three times from other parishes and neighborhoods undergoing racial change. The music director has found a natural way to bring in a Hispanic choir and an African American choir from two other parishes to sing regularly with his. One is from the parish for which his parish takes up a monthly, sharing collection. The other has the same community of Sisters teaching in its school as in his parish. His choir has also gone to their parishes to sing. Together, they mix music from all these cultures and do it so well that they've taken their act out on the road on a number of occasions. They have even made a tape recording to sell. In a parish that might be expected to exhibit tremendous intolerance of minorities, the choir, through the ministry of its director, has been able to bridge gaps, bring people and cultures together, allow for real dialogue, and not tolerate any racist comments or attitudes. Humble and caring, but focused as to what his calling as music director entails, this fine man preaches Jesus loudly and clearly.

In a society that grows frighteningly more compartmentalized and turned in on itself, we must fight those same urges in ourselves. For, at the same time our world is growing smaller. When we help others reach outside of their own concerns to become conscious of the needs of their sisters and brothers and willing to act on them, it is then that we have, by rendering to Caesar what is his also rendered to God all that belongs to God. It is our loving reaching out to others beyond our own circle that will help them to be able to love others as well and that is what the church should be all about.

CHAPTER 11

"Is it lawful to work a cure on the Sabbath?"

Breaking the rules

NOT every person involved with visiting people in the hospital is ready to admit that he or she has experienced the following scenario, or something similar to it. But if one brings the Eucharist and the prayers of the concerned community to the sick often enough, there is a good chance that it has occurred or will in the near future. For some ministers when it does happen, it becomes a time of tremendous guilt and confusion. For others it becomes an opportunity to act out their anti-institutional anger and disobedience. And fortunately for others, it will become a very natural outgrowth of their work, a part of their loving the people of God to whom they find themselves called to serve.

One woman has shared her journey through similar stages in moving fashion. She remembers the first time a hospitalized parishioner asked her to hear his confession before giving him Communion, she was stunned and embarrassed. And in her confusion she actually reminded him not only that she was not a priest, but also that she was a woman, in case he hadn't noticed. She then used the phone at the bedside of the patient to call a priest to come and take care of the matter. Certainly she left the room not at all pleased with her response to this difficult situation. Over time her attitude and response in similar situations made her resentful of the restrictions the church put on her ministry simply because she was female. In her frustration and rage she found herself actively engaging hospitalized parishioners in such a way that they would ask for reconciliation from her before she would give them the Eucharist. Being a loving person, this solution proved totally unsatisfying to her and more than a little troublesome. Working with her spiritual director she was able to grow more confident in the importance of her role as minister of Care. This allowed her to be more focused when she was asked by patients to hear their confessions. She told them calmly that she was not a priest. She would then help them to pray and to privately come to a measure of reconciliation with God. Then, if they were comfortable, she gave them the Eucharist. While this approach was successful in some cases, she was still bothered by the fact that many of the patients were left confused and some would not receive Communion.

If she was bringing people the Eucharist, why could she not lead them to reconciliation with that same God? It took the wisdom and the faith of a ninety-seven-year-old Polish woman to answer her question. The elderly lady took her hands after hearing her explanation as to why she could not hear her confession. She told her that she knew that she would never be leaving the hospital and that anyone who was good and kind enough to bring her Jesus in Communion could also bring her Jesus' forgiveness. Then she began the familiar formula for the Sacrament of Reconciliation but instead of saying "Bless me, Father," she prayed "Bless me, friend." It was then that the woman became comfortable with listening when some patients asked her to hear their confessions. She understood that their faith ordained her at those moments. She would no longer fight it.

Some people will read this description of what had naturally evolved in her life and identify with it comfortably. Others will be shocked and outraged. After all, she is not a priest. She should not be acting like one. She is wrong, plain and simple. She must stop and most probably she should even no longer be allowed to serve as a Minister of Care because she has abused her function.

We need to remember that Pharisees were (and are) not bad people, really. More often than not they just get so hung up on the letter of the law that they begin to live to keep the law rather than to love others. They cannot put love ahead of law, compassion ahead of regulation, people ahead of statutes. When the Pharisees around Jesus remained more concerned about the fact that a law constructed by humans was broken because a person was cured on the Sabbath than able to rejoice in the fact that a fellow human being who was once sick and in pain, frightened and alone, was mercifully cured, made healthy and whole, we can begin to see the terrible effect preoccupation with the law can have on others and on us. And those Pharisees are still around. Is the pastor who will baptize no illegitimate babies or the pastoral associate who takes no calls after 4:00 PM, or the deacon who demands envelope use before marrying a couple any different? Hardly. Those are all human rules and regulations often more for the benefit of the law maker rather than for the people in need of healing.

It is more than a little ironic and very sad that so many

of the people who are attracted to the church are those who throughout their training and later exhibit a rigidity that can only be described as Pharisaical. Let's face it. Just how many open, free-spirited bishops are there? And what usually happens to them? But before we engage in any hierarchy bashing, all we need to do is to look around at those who are involved in the church with us. What we will see all too often are some very rigid and controlling people. The church too often attracts many who need to manipulate and lord it over others because of their own insecurities. And they do it by totally accepting and enforcing an absolutely unbending and uncompromisingly rigid code of law. From a Cardinal Ratzinger in Rome summoning theologians to trial, to the lector who refuses to change a sexist word at the Sunday Morning Liturgy, such attitudes permeate the church today. It is frightening. But it is also no wonder that people are choosing to stay away from this kind of church because in this church there is no way that loving the people of God can take place. The law stands rigidly apart and above people and relationships. And unfortunately this problem is not just the church's. In today's society it is prevalent in most institutions because institutions are growing more dependent on laws and regulations and less on relationships. Remember the picture of Dan Berrigan smiling and handcuffed, captured after years of eluding the F.B.I.? Remember the dour expressions on the faces of the agents who were carrying him off? Clearly here was a person whose love of people liberated him from the law. It also showed the heaviness of the law burdening down those who had chosen to enforce it. The law doesn't necessarily set us free.

Dominic Grassi

If we who are involved in the church genuinely love the people whom we serve, then they become more important to us than any set of rules or regulations. This means that often we become buffers between the laws that are written coldly in black and white and the human persons who need, above all else, to be listened to and affirmed by us. That puts us in the middle. If we aren't willing to be there, then we betray our identity and lose all credibility. Even more, this also means there are times we look at the rules and not so much ignore them as decide that they do not bind us. This is not bending them or trying to get around them or hoping it is not noticed. No, it means that there are times when we must break the laws of the very institutions that we represent because the people we serve are more important to us than the institution we serve. We serve those who are part of the body of Christ and not a corporate structure. This does not make us traitors as some would call us. By serving the people ultimately we best serve the institution, for they are the very reason the institution exists.

Any priest who has ever used the "internal forum" and bypassed the Marriage Tribunal and witnessed a marriage that could otherwise have been delayed for a year or two by intrusive red tape or perhaps never approved, understands. The pastoral associate who counsels a couple to consider ways perhaps not accepted by *Humanae Vitae* to plan their family know what we must do at times. The lector who politely but firmly refuses to be scheduled to read Paul's words about women being submissive to their husbands finds herself in the same category. Fortunately, prudent personal choices and decisions to go against laws and regulations in certain pastoral

146

situations and made in private are often not difficult for the compassionate person to make.

Unfortunately, there are those who call themselves Christians who find responding to people in strict legalistic ways extremely easy. There are many who create laws and rules that go beyond the church's public position. The pastor who refuses to baptize a "bastard" because the parents are not married or because even if they are married they are not using their weekly envelopes is abusing his role by setting himself up as judge rather than minister. The same holds true for the deacon who invades an engaged couple's privacy by demanding to know their views on birth control. Among the worst offenders are those who teach the young and impressionable the Faith as if it were only rules to be kept. Why do people do this? Perhaps it is for power or because of their own personal demons. Perhaps they need to surround themselves in a rigid, protective envelope that allows them to survive. Who knows? But it is because of this that people are sadly or angrily leaving the church. It is because of them that we must never be afraid to respond in love to people. Sadly, we have to provide a counterbalance. As one pastoral associate put it, "Much of my work is picking up the pieces of peoples' lives that priests have shattered with their lack of consideration and compassion."

It is no wonder that people are starting to "shop around" for a parish or worshipping community that will be receptive to them and their needs. When a parish or a staff or an individual develops a reputation for being open and compassionate they are quickly accused of promoting a "McDonald's" style of "fast food" Christianity, of making it "too easy" on people. It is upsetting to both the rigid and the lazy. And so those who love people and respond to them with that love are accused of being wrong or unorthodox. Instead, we are supposed to make it tough on people. We shouldn't be afraid to judge them. If they are uncomfortable or if they squirm, it's their problem, not ours, not the church's. It is no wonder that church attendance and affiliation continue to shrink even as the Pharisees sit in empty rectories, preach to empty pews, and gather to congratulate each other on preserving the true faith.

The couple in charge of baptismal preparation in a small parish welcomed the parents and their child warmly, expressing joy that the beautiful two-year-old was finally going to be baptized. But they quickly found out that the former pastor before his transfer to a larger, more prestigious parish had refused to baptize the child because the mother was not Catholic. The sad irony was that the mother had strongly desired to join the church. The former pastor had given her a four hundred-page book and told her when she was done reading it to come back and he would decide if he would baptize her and her baby. His response should anger anyone. The concerned couple took all the time necessary to bring about the genuine healing that was needed. And ultimately after a number of private sessions, the mother eagerly entered the R.C.I.A. program. Though not directly involved, they monitored her progress and ultimately both mother and child were baptized at the Easter Vigil. The mother and her husband are now actively involved in one parish, thinking about the parish school for their child. Good and loving care and concern will bring people back to the church. And that is more

DO YOU LOVE ME?

important than any set of rules or regulations created by either a distant hierarchy or by the local authority.

There are times when we need to go public and openly disagree with authority. And like the person who is sometimes compelled to become prophet, it is never done lightly or without prayer and reflection. Far from undermining authority, such actions provide the needed forums for the legitimate discussion of issues. Disagreement, as some of the U.S. bishops attempted to explain to the totally perplexed Pope on his last visit, does not mean disloyalty. Many years ago, the first priests who were courageous enough to refuse to wait until after white parishioners had received Communion to give it to their African American parishioners were often times breaking rules set up by their bishops. Nuns who took up banners and marched in the South for civil rights were often breaking their communities' rules as well as local municipal laws. The priest who climbs a missile site fence to protest nuclear warheads often does so without approval from his congregation. The pastoral team attempting to work with gay religious men and women are often not allowed to speak publicly in some dioceses. The local parish that provides sanctuary for oppressed Central Americans is breaking many laws. All of them will be labeled by some people in the church as troublemakers, as heretics, as poor Christian examples.

Recently, when the Chicago City Council was attempting to pass a Human Rights Ordinance to protect vulnerable minority groups, the archdiocese came out publicly and officially against it because by protecting the rights of those who were gay, it might compromise the archdiocesan hiring and firing of employees or possibly appear as condoning their lifestyle. And so the official church would not be supportive, especially with the current pronouncements issuing from Rome. Many pastoral ministers in parishes with significant gay populations stood with their people in supporting the ordinance despite strong pressure from "downtown." Other churches from around the city joined in support as well. The ordinance passed and the concerns that the chancery expressed have not surfaced. Many aldermen with large Catholic constituencies expressed their gratitude for words and notes of encouragement that came to them from many local parishes and their staff. Some may argue that the church must take the position it does on many issues because it represents a larger constituency and sees the larger picture. It should also be argued that individuals in their love for the people they are with and who they serve must take the positions that they do.

One very large concern remains, given the current structure of the church today. It is much harder and much more of a risk for those who are employed by the church but not ordained to be so public and so vocal in their protests. The bottom line is that they can be and often are, fired. There is a genuine lack of justice in the system as it now exists. Many courageous but non-ordained people have become martyrs for their beliefs. On the other hand, priests are seldom if ever removed from the priesthood. They might be called in and read the riot act but only occasionally are they transferred or silenced. That is why clergy must be willing to stand with others who have so much more to lose even if it may affect their reputation or standing with the powers that be.

DO YOU LOVE ME?

The administration of a cluster of parishes in a predominantly African-American area of the city was repeatedly chastised for not sending the Chancery the figures for baptism and weddings and funerals in the cluster. A man with tremendous love and commitment to his people and to those he served refused to do so because his staff had convinced him that those figures did not accurately reflect the work that they were doing in the community. By asking for those figures and nothing else about the work going on in the area, the powers that be could conceivably use that information as the reason for closing a number of the churches and curtailing church efforts in the area. Finally, he was called down to the Chancery Office. He was led to believe that he was going to a one-on-one meeting with a sympathetic Vicar. Instead, he found himself sitting at a large oval table facing an array of diocesan officials.

Clearly, it was an attempt to intimidate him. But it backfired. Instead of frightening him, the meeting only served to anger him and make him more resolute. They had played their strongest hand. Being a priest, there was little more that they would choose to do to him. Ultimately when his term of office was up, they did embarrass him by terminating his assignment four months earlier than scheduled, a mere slap on the wrist. A lay administrator would not have survived as long.

In the church, we seldom, if ever, deal with black and white, right or wrong. More often we are dealing with perceptions, with relationships, with consciences, in short, with people. Most of us who choose to go against authority because of our love for people do so prayerfully and painfully. We

151

Dominic Grassi

are not sociopaths who gleefully undermine authority. Neither are we radicals intent on dismantling the church. We love the church because the Church is the People of God, the mystical Body of Christ. Our intent is not to change dogma or destroy the institution. We are loving and faith-filled and good people.

There are times, however, when enough is enough and we act with no little anger at what has been handed down to us from on high in the form of rules that we are expected to enforce without question. How many teachers in classrooms, how many counselors in the privacy of their offices, how many youth ministers who know and deal with the young are going to simply accept the U.S. bishop's latest statements about AIDS and condoms? The bishops have so obviously and embarrassingly disagreed and flipflopped on this issue—seemingly all with one eye on Rome—that they have lost their credibility. And make no mistake about it, law without credibility is powerless. In this case the anger lies in their realization that it is not the bishops (whose adamant statements will ultimately lead to unwanted pregnancies, disease, heartbreak, and even death) who will be the ones who will have to deal with the people so affected. Many good but human people will suffer. And it will be those of us who love and care for the people who will try to counsel and comfort them as best we can. And sadly, our anger will become real and just because of the bishops' position.

In other cases, the so-called rules or laws or regulations are so obviously out of sync with reality that they are quickly forgotten. Do Eucharistic Ministers pay attention to the admonition in the bulletin that the Eucharist is only for the bap-

DO YOU LOVE ME?

tized Catholics in the congregation? Or does anyone remember Rome's statement from a while back that priests should always dress in public in clerical garb? I wonder what the Pope wears as he goes skiing down the Italian alps? Sometimes it all verges on the comical.

Choices are never easy. And it is good that they aren't. Perhaps they shouldn't be. To act in a particular way simply because it is perceived as the radical or liberal position is just as rigid as unbending legalism and just as dangerous because once again the people are no longer the central focus. Our actions should consistently be based on our belief in what it means to serve others. It means to love them, nothing less. After a fairly rowdy wedding rehearsal, the bride-to-be asked if the priest could give everyone there some sort of absolution so that the bridal party and family of some fifty or so could receive communion at the wedding Mass the next day. What were the available responses? "No," because there doesn't appear to be any real repentance among them? Or, "let them come to Confession at the usual time that it is offered," or, "no, there's too many of you to hear individual confessions at this late hour?" Or, "no, sorry, communal absolution is not allowed?" Or, "okay, since the law allows it since there is only one priest here and so many of you?" Or, "let's kneel here for a minute and reflect on God's love that will be celebrated tomorrow. Let's take this opportunity to reflect on our own lives and ask God to forgive us those times we have not loved and we should have." Which choice would be that of someone who genuinely desires to use the opportunity to bring people back home to God and the church?

Dominic Grassi

To be church is to love others. To heal others we must love them. Not to heal them, not to love them because of a particular rule or regulation is an abdication of what we are called to do. What are we afraid of beyond losing the power these rules and regulations give us over people? Really, we don't need any more power than loving others gives us. That's a powerful love. That's a perfect love. We should aim for such perfect love because there will and can never be a perfect law. And so each in our own way, we must continue when the situation arises to choose to work cures on the Sabbath.

CHAPTER 12

"Could you not stay awake?"

Burnout

A GROUP of pastors, all under forty-five, met on a brisk fall Sunday evening. It was a monthly support group that came together because of common concerns. At this particular meeting they admitted to being more than a little tired and frustrated and not a little frightened about the future. For one of them, Mass attendance was declining and he was taking it personally. For another, racial change and the ensuing violence had begun to develop in his parish boundaries. For still another, the diocese had withdrawn a promised loan on a needed church renovation project that he had begun. Others in the group also listed their woes. As the evening wore on, anger with "downtown" became more and more the focus of the group. Only in the final moments of the evening did they share with each other some of the positive "sparks" they had been able to light and the appreciation and gratitude shown to them by some of the people. The meeting ended without having resolved anything for any of them. Perhaps some of them were able to go back to their rectories a little less frustrated, with at least a feeling of some solidarity with the others. But they knew beyond that things were not much different than before the meeting.

Ironically, at the same time that this meeting was happening, the president of the parish pastoral council and the president of the parish school board of one of the other pastor's parishes were meeting. And they, too, spoke of their own frustrations and concerns. They felt that the pastor was not involved nearly enough in the school and needed to spend more time there because of problems that had arisen with the principal and with some of the teachers. They were certain that he needed to be more involved with the people. In their eyes, he wasn't responsive enough. Others were complaining to them and so the two of them were feeling the pressures of their positions. Yet none of this had been, nor would be shared with the pastor.

At just about the same time as all this was happening, members of the finance committee of that parish were being overwhelmed and demoralized by a few, isolated negative responses to an ongoing fundraising effort. Parishioners were not understanding, not wanting to understand the reasons and motives behind the drive.

The night before, the principal of the grammar school had missed a school board annual fundraiser and party because she was simply too exhausted to attend after an exceptionally tough week in school. She felt guilty and knew there would be criticism.

An usher/greeter, meanwhile, thought that by adding additional ushers at the Masses that weekend the pastor was no longer happy with his and others of the old-time ushers' performance and so was going to fire them. And he was spreading that rumor to them all.

So, what do we have going on here? Is this a parish in

complete disarray? Is there no effective leadership in it? Is this the beginning of the end? Probably not. More than likely, it is a good parish where many good things are happening and where a great deal of genuine, loving concern is shared by many dedicated people. If there is a problem, it is that perhaps too much is being attempted too quickly. And so many, if not all of those involved in the parish are at the beginning stage of what could ultimately grow into a serious burnout problem.

Jesus' public ministry lasted a scant three years, not very long at all. In that short period of time, he selected his disciples and attempted to show and to teach them not only who he was and what kind of messiah he would be, but also what the church he was leaving to them should be. More often than not he moved too quickly for them. They couldn't keep up with him. It was all too much for them. Consistently, they misunderstood him and so found themselves responding to him in a way that received a gentle rebuke. Or, to his dismay, they would do the wrong thing. It is no wonder at all, then, that the very wine which he shared with them at the Last Supper would also become the catalyst for their falling asleep at the very cusp of the Resurrection event. They were unable to stay awake and pray. They were unable to rise to the culmination of Jesus' life, to the events that ushered in the very birth of the church. It was all beyond their comprehension and their energies. They were incapable of handling it and so they ran from it and hid in their sleep. They were frightened, no doubt, by what Jesus had just shared with them. But also, after three years they were also tired, confused, and, in short, burntout. There hadn't been enough time for them to prepare to be and to do all that had been expected of them.

Some two thousand years later, the church has not really changed that much. There is still so much, too much, for us to do and nowhere near enough time in which to do it. And, more often than not, there are not enough resources available to do it right. So, stretched as far as we can be stretched, we try to do and try to be a little bit more until, without warning something inside of us pops. Suddenly out pours all the bitterness from all the hurts we have endured, great and small. The insecurities that were lying just beneath the surface at the same time become magnified. We find ourselves in retreat, literally leaving many of our tasks undone or half-finished, or we retreat figuratively, through passionless motions, busying ourselves more and more with other concerns. We have tried as hard as we could. Perhaps we have tried too hard and in the process we have hurt ourselves. And we suffer like the people around us. It is no easy task to attempt to love unconditionally.

These days it is fashionable to speak and write about burn-out. It is almost as fashionable to describe ourselves as so busy and hardworking that we most probably are on the brink of burn-out. But we go on, heroically dedicated. Really, all we are doing is looking for some needed recognition that we are working hard. In reality, those who really are burntout do not talk about it proudly. They don't usually talk about it at all. Usually they are hurt, quiet, sullen: often they have an anger bubbling beneath the surface because they feel that they are not and have not been appreciated and that their work has all been done in vain.

There is a saying I found in a small book of Italian proverbs that translates loosely, "I'm the one who's peeling the onions and you are the one crying." Most knowledgeable old Italians will be quick to tell you that this book sanitized the more vividly colorful expression. "I'm the one laying the eggs and you are the one complaining of a sore backside." All too often those who are complaining the loudest about all that they are doing are in reality the ones who are doing the least. Make no mistake about it. They take good care of themselves. On the other hand, all too often the good and conscientious prople working with love and compassion are the ones who find themselves gradually overwhelmed by it all, drained and emptied.

In quiet desperation, a parish social worker calls a friend frustrated and in tears. She had met with five clients that day and she had been able to help them all. But the bureaucracy and the red tape had worn her down and caught up with her. She was completely unable to see the good that she had done that day. All she wanted to do was to quit then and there. She would feel better in the morning, but not much.

The first sign of burn-out in the church is the inability to appreciate the mystery of God's choosing to work through us. Because most of the rewards of our work are internal and come from our own vision and faith, we need to be able to appreciate the good that we do even when others do not. At the same time, it is most important to be able to take those occasional notes, compliments, and words of gratitude and to savor them because they come so few and far between. But when we burn out, we tend to hear more of the negative, those things that make it harder to continue. And the good is somehow lost. The less we feel appreciated, the less we are able to appreciate the work we are doing and the less we choose to do it with conviction.

Rather than interpreting additional volunteer help in the office as both a way of expanding the program and also as recognition that her importance went beyond the secretarial tasks she was performing, a Director of Religious Education found herself growing very bitter and sarcastic. She directed this at the pastor who tried to line up more help for her, the people who made so many demands on her, and, most unfortunately, at the children to whom she had been so committed. More and more, she set herself apart from them all and began to pass judgment on them with great ease.

The second sign of burn-out is a growing sarcasm and callousness. Moving from loving people to pitying them and finally to mocking them can happen quickly, and, unfortunately, quite easily. Often the choice is either to grow angry with the people whom we serve or to laugh at them because of the demands their humanity places on us. At first, such feelings are kept private. After a while they grow into comments that are shared with a select few. And when we find ourselves frazzled, tired, and feeling unappreciated we explode at people, or, worse yet, make cold, cruel, and cutting comments. Burntout, we can no longer respect and so can no longer love those who have opened themselves up to us. Our burn-out causes tremendous pain and hurt.

At a scheduled Parent/Teacher Conference at a Catholic

DO YOU LOVE ME?

High School, parents were lined up in the hall and called into the classroom two by two to meet with the teachers and talk about their child's progress. A couple came in and expressed to the teacher some concerns about their son's behavior toward another student. The frustrated and uptight teacher referred to the other student as a "little bastard." On completion of that session with the parents the next couple walked into the classroom. Imagine the teacher's surprise and embarrassment when they angrily introduced themselves as the parents of "the little bastard" you were just talking about." They had overheard the teacher. There was little he could now say or do that would be productive and caring. His sarcasm and anger had surfaced at the wrong time. He was unable to control it. He could, therefore, no longer deal with them effectively.

A third sign of burn-out is when its concerns, tensions, and frustrations spill over so much into our private lives that they indeed are no longer private. This is not only a problem for the priest who may be living "over the shop." But it is also a problem for all those who juggle jobs, relationships, children and many other commitments with their service. There comes a time when everyone in church work needs to realize that it is okay for an outside concern to take precedent without their feeling at all guilty about it.

We are not called to be martyrs. When the disarray of our involvement (it seldom is orderly) pours over into our private lives to such a degree that it all begins to overwhelm us, the natural instinct and tendency is to back away. Unfortunately, we then find ourselves feeling ever more guilty. So we throw ourselves back into it full force and risk serious burnout.

161

Dominic Grassi

For one mother, what began simply as volunteering on an occasional Saturday to bring the Eucharist to a few elderly shut-ins quickly and unexpectedly developed into co-ordinating ten or twelve others who had volunteered to help out as well. It also meant she filled in for them when they had other commitments. Now, not only was every Saturday lost to anything but ministry—meaning she could no longer attend her son's football games or her daughter's gymnastic meets—but also, the rest of her week was rapidly filling up. There were phone calls from needy but pesky shut-ins that would lead to five or six extra trips to the supermarket. And there were calls that had to be made to family members appraising them of issues or concerns regarding their shut-in relative. It's no wonder that her children grew jealous and her husband sullen. She felt more and more burdened by it all. But she also felt trapped. The work had to be done. The shut-ins wouldn't just disappear. Burn-out was setting in.

There are many symptoms of burn-out that may or may not appear in individual situations. They include: physical illness, psychosomatic illness, personality change, no time for friends, the inability to relax, a decrease in inner resources available to deal with solvable problems, mood swings where the highs are too high and the lows too low, the inability to reflect and pray. Any combination of these may point to the increased probability of burn-out. There is no doubt that everyone experiences some of these symptoms, and others as well, at some time or another. It's an occupational hazard. And that is why genuine burn-out can sneak up on us. We need to constantly monitor ourselves. At the same time, we need to love each other enough to look out for one another.

DO YOU LOVE ME?

There are times when we need to be the ones ministered to, either by a co-minister or by someone we have been serving. There is nothing wrong with this healthy transference. In fact, the revelation of our very humanness and our limitations may allow us ultimately to grow closer to others than we might have expected and so too at a future date be able to help them in an even more beautiful way.

We need to remember that we are all unique persons with unique capabilities and needs. We are not and must never be in competition with each other. And that means we do not let ourselves be drawn into the "numbers game" counting the people we serve with one eye while checking the bottom line to see if we are somehow winning the race. No matter what we feel, no matter what others expect of us, there is no right number of people to counsel in a week, no quota of ill to visit in the hospitals or in their homes. If another person, for whatever reason, is capable of doing more than we are, that is fine for them. We should support them. There is absolutely no reason for us to feel guilty. We can only do what we are capable of doing and no more or less.

An administrator of a large Catholic educational institution was always scheduling meetings for late into the night and over holidays and weekends. Those of his staff were expected to share his vision and keep up with him. Many had good intentions but tired. And many fell by the wayside. He remained single-minded in his demands. It wasn't until his own father became seriously ill and he found that he had to adjust his schedule frequently and be available to his family and so limit the time he could give to his tasks as minister, that he realized how unfair it had been for him to demand that others with their own family and personal concerns be expected to do all that he had been driving himself to do. He still works very hard but he has grown more accepting of other staff members' levels of involvement.

Priests especially need to be cautioned to be open and sensitive to the private lives of those with whom they work. It's too easy to forget that they have other concerns and responsibilities, that their lives are more than their work. Phone calls at all hours of the day or night, taking them away from their family by forgetting that holidays are family days, not realizing that they have other obligations can lead the most generous and giving of people to the edge of burn-out and, if we are not careful, over that edge. Not only has the church lost good people, but we cannot calculate the hurt and pain that it has caused them and their families.

How to prevent such burn-out or at least to survive it intact has already been hinted at in the pages of this book. We need to remember that we are not messiahs. For many of us that is no easy lesson to learn or to accept. No matter how hard we try, we cannot save everyone who comes to us for help every time. To believe we can smacks of real arrogance. We will and we do make mistakes and because of them we will hurt people. There is no way around that fact. We will watch helplessly as people hurt themselves and be unable to stop them. Putting it bluntly, if we can't handle these realities then perhaps we are not called to be involved in the church to the degree we are. We never want to grow callous, but at the same time we have to accept the facts. Perhaps we could find other ways of volunteering our time and generosity that won't involve us in the lives of others. This may sound

DO YOU LOVE ME?

harsh, but ministry means taking risks with people. And taking risks means we're not always going to succeed. Our faith must make us ready to accept that.

I learned this painfully the hard way. While in the seminary, I was asked by a court-appointed psychologist to work with a teenager who had a number of scrapes with the law because of his experimenting with drugs. Puffing his pipe solemnly, the psychologist intoned gravely that I was the teenager's last hope. How could I resist such a challenge? I spent weeks trying to develop a relationship with a rebellious teenager who had no interest at all in meeting with some do-gooder who was going to be a priest someday. Everything culminated on a snowy afternoon when he jumped out of the passenger side of my car—we were going forty miles an hour. Fortunately, he landed in a recently plowed snowdrift. Actually, I was more hurt than he was. It was just about the clearest sign of rejection I could ever experience. I went crawling to my spiritual director moaning and groaning all about it, expecting solace, or at least a pat on the head. Instead, he grew visibly angry with me and my feeling sorry for myself. He challenged me. How dare I be so presumptuous, so full of myself to think that I or anyone could be anyone's last hope! I had given it my best shot and I had been rejected. It wouldn't be the last time. And he helped me to see that the sooner I could learn that this is the way life is the better it would be for me. Talk about a double dose of reality therapy.

A second source for help has already been mentioned. It is imperative that we be supportive of each other in any way that we can. We need to watch out for each other. We need to support each other. We need to help each other out. We can cover for each other. We can ask for help from each other. We can challenge each other to take it easy and to back off. We can help each other to laugh and put things in their proper perspective. We can be a comforting shoulder to cry on when necessary. We can be an ear to listen to frustrations being poured out. And we can give a warm embrace that will make it better. But clearly, we cannot be isolated individuals just doing our own ministerial thing, occasionally bumping into each other almost by accident. If we love each other then we can and will help each other.

A tired and discouraged pastoral minister was invited to another staff member's home for dinner. Upon his arrival, he was handed a frosty strawberry margarita, guided to a hammock under an apple tree, and given a Walkman with the soundtrack from *The Mission* in it. He was then gently ordered to relax and told that dinner would be ready in an hour. It had been clear to many people that he desperately needed some time to relax and unwind. And so that couple who worked side by side with him, and cared for him, decided to provide it for him. It's hard to burn out with that kind of support around you.

Earlier in this book, the importance of prayer and spiritual guidance and direction was emphasized for different reasons. It's fitting to repeat that message here as well. If we allow ourselves the time and distance to be nourished by our faith and by our relationship with God who loves us, all that we are doing and all our concerns can be put into a healthier perspective. The quiet time of prayer and reflection and meditation will not only help our souls, it will also allow our psyches and bodies to heal as well. Prayer can also help us to keep in perspective the fact that we are not alone in the church. Rather, we realize that we are the instrument by which our God will reach others. God is always with us.

Remember the pastoral counselor who moved from occasionally praying for a case or a person with whom she was working to praying before each session with a client, to now inviting the client to pray with her at the start of their session. She is exhibiting a growing awareness of the presence of God in her work. She feels that prayer helps focus her. It gives her confidence and it allows her to deal better with both failures and successes.

Finally, we must be honest enough and have the courage to know when it is time to step away from what we are doing or even to leave it all behind and get on with our lives in another direction. Time off and away, retreats and vacations are necessary if we are to remain able to keep all we do in perspective. But there might also come the time when we have to decide to pack our bags and leave the work that we have been doing for others. We know that we've given it our best shot and that there is no more to give. It is time to let someone else try. It's not time for sadness, but rather for rejoicing. We have had the opportunity to enter people's lives, to touch them, to love them. If we are lucky, we have formed some lasting friendships. We don't want to wait until it's too late and then decide to leave.

I recently visited the village in which my father was born in South Central Italy. A small church stands in the center of the town. Don Pietro has been the pastor for well over eighteen years. He is a good, decent, hardworking man. But given the fact that the culture is very anticlerical, the amount of criticism directed toward him still seemed inordinately severe. He was there whenever people needed him. Naturally over the years he had to make some tough and unpopular decisions. He had a history with most of the people or at least with their families. Over lunch I asked him in Italian how long he intended to stay on as pastor. With a sad shrug of his hands he asked where else could he go. He felt that he was too old to move. How sad! It was no longer good for him or for the people.

The hardest part of our work is leaving the people we love. But if we understand what love really means, we know that there will have to be a time to let go. Even Jesus felt the pain. "The birds have their nests and the foxes their lairs, but the Son of Man has no place to lay his head." Burn-out will happen when we hang on too long, afraid not only of what we might lose when we let go, but also afraid of what the future will hold for us. We always need to be challenged. When we no longer are, we have in effect stopped being church.

So, let us realize and accept the fact that we cannot do it all. We have neither the time, the talent or the energy. When we are asked why we could not stay awake, we don't have to be defensive and chop off somebody's ear. Let our answer not be because we have been overwhelmed by all we are called to do and be. Let us rather say we slept because we have prayerfully chosen with the advice and support of our friends to take the necessary break that will ultimately make us better Christians.

CHAPTER 13

"What can a person offer in exchange for life?"

A choice of rewards

EVERY day I have an encounter with a ghost, one Francis Xavier Lange, to be more specific. His stern visage is set larger than life into the stained glass transom over the center aisle vestibule door of the church that he built back in 1900. He wasn't the parish's first pastor. He was the third, the second having lasted all of one week. (And we think things are bad today!) He is not the last either. I came in seven after him. But in the history of the parish he's the one who stands out larger than life. Stories about him abound. On the evening of his arrival at the parish, he found a mob of seven hundred angry parishioners storming the convent (Sister Superior had somehow appeared to them as supportive of an associate pastor who had run off with parish funds. School Board meetings are calm by comparison, these days.) He dispersed the crowd and so began his remarkable tenure.

His bilingual homilies (Kashube and Polish) were legendary. From the high pulpit he would tell the one group that the other was doing more for the parish than they were, and weren't they ashamed? Then he would switch languages and say the same thing to the other group. It is no wonder that he was able to build the first fireproof Catholic Church in the United States—twice! A cyclone hit the area and knocked down the structure as it was being built. And there was no insurance. He just started over again. Once it was built he led parishioners on nighttime raids to tear up railroad tracks that were being laid on the street in front of the new church during the day. (Talk about community activism!) The railroad company finally gave in and moved the tracks two blocks east where they remain to this day. It was said that old Frank rejected several opportunities to be named a bishop. (Wise man.) It is no wonder that ten thousand people were in attendance at his funeral; he was loved.

It was an easier time to be involved in the church back then. At least, that's what I tell myself. Everyday I walk down the aisle of that church he built, look up at Frank's face and ask him how I'm doing. I fully suspect that one of these days he's going to smile. Until then, I'll just have to make do. On bad days I ask myself and Frank, "Why am I doing this?" On good days, I just toss him a wave.

Let's face it. There are very few heroes around in our world and even fewer martyrs. We who work in the church better not include ourselves in either group. When we are honest with ourselves, we realize that the one reason we are able to continue to serve the People of God is that we enjoy what we are doing. Nobody is forcing us to do what we do. We are not unlike the rest of humanity. Like any of those who are blessed with freedom as we are, we do what we're doing because we find it rewarding and fulfilling. We need to beware of the temptation to impress others, hoping that they will join ranks with us, by presenting the church as some kind of heroic and holy grail that we have nobly and bravely

170

undertaken to pursue. It doesn't wash. Most people can see through our false bravado. Others will be attracted to the church by seeing us happy and whole in our work. The fact is, if we are not fulfilled, we will not be effective in our work no matter how much we try to impress others.

All of us have been invited by Jesus to be ministers. His invitation is really a loaded question. He asks us what can we offer in exchange for life, for all the blessings he has given to us? Immediately, we all know that the only answer is life itself. Nothing else will do. For some reason, the question is not asked of everyone. Somehow by hearing the question, we have already begun to respond to it because hearing the question means that we have already began to give ourselves to the people who are the very means by which Jesus asks us the question. Hearing Jesus, hearing the question are those who have said yes, who continue to say yes, and are comfortable with those choices.

If we think that our work is going to be instantly appreciated in such a way that everyone to whom we minister is going to gratefully support us, we will quickly learn how wrong we can be. It just doesn't happen that way. A lector can proclaim the Word of God flawlessly for months, but one mispronounced Old Testament location will provoke all too many comments. A pastoral associate can put more than eighty hours a week into her parish, but if she misses one sodality meeting because her car broke down, the old timers will loudly complain that a "real" priest would not have missed their meeting. A deacon can work hard at setting up and implementing a new marriage preparation program only to be told that he's not the same guy he used to be because it cost him the opportunity to play poker with the Holy Name men. We are public figures. And the people we are trying to serve, God love them, like to talk and gossip and complain. And sometimes that talk unfortunately is small. And sometimes that unfortunate small talk gets back to the minister. Make no mistake. It hurts.

So why do we continue what we are doing for the church? What is in it that brings us joy and happiness and a sense of genuine satisfaction? Why take the risks that seem to be built into the job?

First of all, we are called to it through those same people who may let us down. We are attracted to serve them. And through it all, we must realize that there is support and affection for us out there. We need to take the time for it. Remember, if we are on the verge of burning out, it becomes difficult, if not impossible, to accept the positive support offered to us. It is then that we are in trouble. For the sake of the good we can do, we can't let that happen.

I'll bet that in the middle of all our phone messages, bills, junk mail and other items that clutter our desks rests a thank-you note. It may be from a grateful couple whose baby we've helped them to prepare for baptism, or from a family whose grieving we shared, or from the spouse of a person we took the time to visit in the hospital. We can take the note and read it in just a matter of seconds and then toss it away. Or perhaps it would be better to put it aside so that we can read it at a more prayerful and reflective time. It is amazing how restorative a few words can be. The compliment, the thank you doesn't always have to be written. If someone expresses gratitude verbally, we can still store it away in our hearts to bring out and savor at the proper time instead of pooh-poohing it out of our thoughts. It is amazing that we almost feel guilty when people want to show us their gratitude. As long as we're not doing what we do in order to elicit such a response from the people, there is nothing wrong. When they do respond to us it can mean a lot.

The premise of this book has been that those of us in the church must love the people whom we serve. There is no doubt that the risk of loving is great. But it is also true that the reward is even greater. We are incredibly blessed. Unlike no one else, we are allowed to enter into the lives of so many people on such intimate levels. We are allowed to love people in a way that no one else can. In fact, our task goes far beyond teaching or sharing, beyond visiting or listening, beyond blessing or preaching. Rather, our task is to love the people in such a way that it compels them to love in response. That love may be given back to us or shared with others. In either case what a great feeling of joy we can have when we bring people to that point of being able to love as we have loved them.

At twenty-eight years old a young man finally quit the un-healthy but lucrative job that he had with his father's com-pany. He would be leaving the next day for an open-ended, extended journey. But before he left, he took the time to visit a priest who had known him and worked with him since high school. His visit had a very specific purpose. It wasn't to thank the priest for all the help that he had given to him over the years, though it had been a substantial amount. Nor was it to thank him for his support and advice when he decided to leave his job. Nor was it to thank him for helping him through the very painful breakup he had experienced with the woman he very nearly had married. Rather, the young man wanted to let the priest know that he, despite all of his own problems and concerns, had been able to help a couple going through some serious problems because of the way the priest had helped him. He was able to love others and minister to them because he felt loved by the priest. The priest, whose travels had not taken him very far from home was deeply touched by the young man's final comment to him as he left to literally go and explore the world. "Don't worry about me," he said. "I'm taking some of you with me. I'll always be okay." If that type of encounter is not fulfilling, nothing is.

The rewards that we receive in ministry can be and are as varied as the work we do. We need to be open to them. The Youth Minister who attends a gathering of others like himself sees a young woman who had been a member of the first teen club he had ever formed a number of years ago. Now she is there as a youth minister herself. They share pleasantries and a few happy memories of those past days. He goes home with a warm feeling. He didn't ask her outright. But perhaps one of the reasons she chose to enter into such work in her life was because of him and his example. That possibility is reward enough for him even if there are no letters of thanks or gratitude.

There are times when no one feels as incredibly alone as we find ourselves. But that is all right. We need to remember that such feelings exist and are enhanced and amplified because none but those who are so involved are able to feel such incredible intimacy with so many people at other mo-

DO YOU LOVE ME?

ments. We would not know the void if we did not know the fullness. The lows certainly become lower because the highs are so incredibly high. Perhaps this realization, when we are down, can be of some consolation.

We need to make the time for two sources of support to be worked into our busy schedules. We first of all need to make the time just to be with and enjoy the company of those whom we are serving. The pastoral associate who chooses never to attend the wedding receptions of the couples she prepared for matrimony; the deacon who never goes to the baptismal parties for the babies he baptized; the co-ordinator of Eucharistic Ministers who never accepts the invitation to stop in and have a cup of coffee with one of the other ministers; the pastor who makes a rule never to go out to eat with any of the parishioners—all are missing opportunities for people to respond in gratitude and in love to them. We have to allow people their way of showing appreciation however they are able. That is an essential part of ministering to them.

Secondly, as has been pointed out numerous times in this book for other reasons, we need to make sure that part of the time we set aside for prayer and reflection becomes time to objectively look and appreciate the good that we are doing. This can be done in private prayers of thanksgiving. Or it can be done in the context of a prayer group discussion with others. We need to realize that sometimes the supports and the rewards we need will remain internal. There will be times that we need to be able to reward ourselves and acknowledge that we have done a good job. Our failures are all too painfully apparent. We must also look at our successes.

All of us know of ministers among us who subconsciously

start substituting possessions for rewards with their wall of testimonial plaques and pictures of themselves with famous people or their fancy office furniture with its trappings of power or the self-importance of a car phone. In the long run these things don't help. In the church there are very few quick rewards or instant gratifications. It takes time to reach people, to nurture a relationship with them, to have them allow us to serve them and to love them. It only stands to reason, then, that it would also take time to know and feel the reward that comes from our work. There can be no quick fix. We cannot be involved in church work for any instant rewards. The work itself and its results often times have to be reward enough. A homily well preached, an adult education program well received, a hymn well sung, a person brought to genuine peace, a mourner truly comforted—these must be reward enough in themselves. The Beatitudes can be translated not only that the peacemakers and comforters are blessed but also more aptly that they are happy. Our ministry should bring us great satisfaction and happiness.

A former seminarian and lifelong teacher, now a permanent deacon, reflected on his quarter century of teaching. The day to day rewards in themselves were not great. Not too many students were deeply interested in Hamlet. Even the number of students who came back later in life to thank him was not all that great either. But seeing how well many of his former students were doing, the few who became priests and those who did not, and knowing that some had even become teachers like himself, that, he felt, is what kept him going.

DO YOU LOVE ME?

But when all is said and done, we should expect no reward at all beyond the profound privilege of being allowed to love so many people. And so we should be enjoying it as much as Jesus must have enjoyed his three years of ministry. He must have enjoyed seeing little Zaccheas scramble down the tree surprised that he had been singled out. He must have enjoyed watching the rocks fall impotently from the hands of those ready to stone the woman caught in adultery. He must have enjoyed feeding the multitude on the hillside. And he really must have enjoyed the meal Peter's mother-in-law served after he cured her. We need to remember always that there could never have been the Resurrection without the Crucifixion, the Agony in the Garden without the Transfiguration. We have to look past the low moments to those great redemptive moments of which we have been privileged to be a part.

The most difficult chapter to write in this book has been this last one on the rewards of a life of service. It is no accident that it is the shortest of the chapters. And it's not because the rewards aren't there. But rather it is because they are so personal. They cannot be weighed or compared or measured by numbers. They cannot be seen in any finished product. They often cannot even be described in words. For those of us who have chosen minstry, the rewards are built into the fabric of the person that we are. They are part of the life we give and share with others. We offer ourselves in love. How can we measure what we receive in exchange?

We are not searching for fame, recognition, money or power. We are compelled by a simple question ''Do you love me?'' to answer with our lives "Yes, and yes again.'' The more we answer that question affirmatively the more that it will be asked of us. We do not just say yes the moment we have been hired, appointed, transferred, selected or ordained. We say yes every time we choose to reach out to others in love. The greatest reward we receive is that our God who loves us with a love that is unconditional will never stop asking us "Do you love me?'' And that is why we continue to minister.